W9-AFT-756

WITHDRAWN

Olive Schreiner

Twayne's World Authors Series

African Literature

Bernth Lindfors, Editor
University of Texas at Austin

TWAS 865

OLIVE SCHREINER

Olive Schreiner

Cherry Clayton

University of Guelph, Ontario

Twayne Publishers
An Imprint of Simon & Schuster Macmillan
New York

Prentice Hall International
London • Mexico City • New Delhi • Singapore • Sydney • Toronto

Twayne's World Authors Series No. 865

Olive Schreiner
Cherry Clayton

Twayne Publishers
An Imprint of Simon & Schuster Macmillan
1633 Broadway
New York, NY 10019

Library of Congress Cataloging-in-Publication Data

Clayton, Cherry.
    Olive Schreiner / Cherry Clayton.
        p.   cm. — (Twayne's world authors series : TWAS 865. African literature)
    Includes bibliographical references and index.
    ISBN 0–8057–8287–7 (alk. paper)
    1. Schreiner, Olive. 1855–1920—Criticism and interpretation.
2. Women and literature—South Africa—History—20th century.
3. Africa, Southern—In literature.   4. South Africa—In literature.
I. Title.   II. Series: Twayne's world authors series : TWAS 865.
III. Series: Twayne's world authors series. African literature.
PR9369.2.S37Z617   1997
823—dc20
                                                    96–36020
                                                    CIP

10 9 8 7 6 5 4 3 2 1

For my mother

Birthday Gift
As I unwrap this parcel, not the first,
and plunge my hands in paper, boxes,
buried birthday gifts, sifting treasure
like the Lucky Dips of childhood—
I want to unpack my love for my mother,
always buried in her element, the flesh,
which does not last but is given to another.

Her tales are of yesterday's bruises, today's
business, the ancient aunt: fretful, fragile, slippery as a
fish when lifted from the bath.
All this and more: deafness, age, vanity,
so-and-so's death or divorce, a grandchild's toys,
the hulking sons whose laundry tumbles in
and out the house, as they once did when boys.

She is my bulky shadow, a whale whose moorings
I never slip, but in whose lee my life passes
like a ship in the dark puzzle of events
whose shape is never clear. I sometimes wear

her clothes, which never fit, but in their
steadying scent all day I know that I
have always been, with her, safe, beloved, dear.

I used to stand on a table and twirl
to the rippling sting of hemline pins
as she snapped and sewed below, another dress
for the party girl. I see us now: separate women
stitched together by the scars of birth, growing older.
I want to record my love, unpack this gift,
before she's gone and the world grows colder.

Contents

Preface

Olive Schreiner's talent has been regarded as both precocious and unfulfilled, her written work somehow not measuring up to the standards she set for herself or those set for her by others; her polemical work has been seen as an unworthy distraction from the unfolding of her creative impulses. Her husband and first biographer, Samuel Cron Cronwright, emphasized the intuitive and childlike aspects of his wife's personality, which were looked upon as bound up with nineteenth-century ideas of "genius." Her lack of a formal education, her impulsive and often irrational behavior, her inability to complete what she had hoped would be a major novel, and an advance on *The Story of an African Farm* (1883) are repeatedly mentioned in her husband's biography and his introductions to posthumous publications. After Cronwright's biography and edition of Schreiner's letters appeared, both of which were based on a limited knowledge of her correspondence and manuscripts, a number of defensive responses arose from admirers and biographers. One of these defenders was Vera Buchanan-Gould, who cast Schreiner in the mold of a victimized woman and female martyr, one who in fact achieved more than could have been expected.[1] Many of Schreiner's own utterances ("I am only a broken and untried possibility")[2] as well as some of her most vivid fictional images of women fed into this view of a Victorian child-genius and invalid.

The fact that Schreiner suffered from almost lifelong asthma is difficult to understand and assess in relation to the body of work she produced and in relation to her life choices and partnerships, including her long but ultimately shipwrecked marriage. It is easy to under- or overestimate the influence of her lifelong asthma, of the drugs she sometimes took to alleviate the asthma, and the relationship between such physiological conditions and her constant changes of residence, her restlessness, her aborted relationships with men, and her difficulties in completing ambitious major studies such as *Woman and Labour* (a fluent but partial reconstruction of a more ambitious project) and *From Man to Man,* the novel she only tinkered with during the last three decades of her life. At the same time she exhibited a compelling image, that of the

contemporary yet lonely and heroic woman artist, which was played out
in her own life and explains many of her apparently disjointed symptoms. She traveled a long way and accomplished a great deal.

Some critics, such as Marion Friedmann[3] and collaborative biographers Ruth First and Ann Scott,[4] have drawn on Freudian theories of
repression, either of her animosity toward her mother and her internalized image of her, or of sexual desire itself, to explain the shape of
Schreiner's life and work. Feminist critic Kathleen Blake[5] has seen in her
life pattern a clear example of the "deferred condition" in which many
women writers have lived. The first modern, scholarly biography of
Schreiner, by Ruth First and Ann Scott, placed her within her historical
context, although one largely construed from a British Marxist perspective, and showed where she attempted a critique of current social and
political conditions in South Africa and England and where she was
blindfolded by the workings of contemporary ideologies, her early reading of Darwin's evolutionary theory, and Herbert Spencer's theory of
humanity's moral perfectibility replacing a belief in a Christian God.[6]
There is no doubt that certain key thinkers blazed across the colonial
sky for her; their hold on her imagination was strong, yet she could say
that she had outgrown Spencer later, as one outgrows a doctor who at
one time sets a broken leg (Rive, 37). One of her concerns is to describe
to the metropolitan world the huge, life-sustaining value of books as
friends to lonely, self-educated colonial youth. Her view of South African
political life and of the position of women developed over time and was
closely bound up with her own experiences inside and outside South
Africa and within her marriage. Her developing feminist vision began to
perceive interrelationships between social structures, colonialism, and
the cultural marginalization of women. As Doris Lessing points out, it is
difficult for us to see Schreiner's views and struggles apart from the
social climate and the behaviors she helped to shape.[7]

The most recent biographical research by South African writer Karel
Schoeman has placed Schreiner fully in relation to South African history
and society; he has accurately established the social context and chronol-
ogy of events and of Schreiner's writings for the first time. In addition,
he has presented a lively and detailed picture of the social scene and
political tensions of each period of her life. Apart from creating an
invaluable research platform for future scholars, he has also used her
writings to illuminate one another, while insisting that the fiction is
almost totally autobiographical, sometimes in a reductive sense. The
distance between Schreiner and her created characters is collapsed quite

ruthlessly in his readings of the novels, and the dimension of any aesthetic ordering of material is lost. First and Scott also write dismissively
of Schreiner's fictions at times, especially when she exhibits sympathy
with the Afrikaner. Thus they describe her Second Anglo-Boer War
story, "Eighteen-Ninety-Nine," which many South Africans justifiably
admire, as "a rather maudlin account of the sufferings of women in
wartime" (First and Scott, 249). Schreiner is viewed as separate from her
writing, but she often claimed that her work was "really me," in the
sense that what she believed and felt was most fully expressed in her
writing. The characters portrayed in her stories were understood as both
separate and integral. The self constructed in the act of writing is never
the same as the self who walks in the street. Her identity was constantly
evolving and drawing energy from her writing.[8] Schreiner's thought
developed organically and was increasingly politicized. The graph of her
oeuvre reflects this growth.

Recent criticism of Schreiner's fiction has drawn on a variety of critical strategies and theories, with much interesting commentary coming
from feminist critics, who continue to engage with the novels and the
nature of her feminism. Rachel Blau Du Plessis, for instance, sees
Schreiner as working innovatively within the genre of the novel, developing feminist narrative strategies to make space for her own voice and
dissenting from social norms by deconstructing certain narrative patterns.[9] Other critics have emphasized the marginal space Schreiner
occupied as a white woman in a colonial culture[10] or have traced the
development of her vision as a process of "healing imagination" respond-
ing to "racist and imperialist poison."[11] Recent critical discussion has
looked closely at the texture of her writing, locating her resistance to
asymmetrical power structures within the "visual cinematic quality"
(Berkman 1989, 228) of her prose or in the "polysemous symbol" of her
fictions.[12] Increasingly, critics have reexamined the dimension of allegory as a key to Schreiner's postcolonial imagination and relationship
with history.[13] Gerald Monsman has revalued her multilayered protest
of the abuses of power prevalent in her time. He writes of her "tough-
minded depiction of the political character of colonialism, the clash
between indigenous ways of life and the march of capitalistic development," locating its source in her "intensely private anguish of the marginalized, especially her own silencing as a colonial woman" (Monsman
1992, 49). The colonial allegory of *The Story of an African Farm,*
Schreiner's most representative text, has now been seen to offer rich
insights into the multiple dispossessions experienced in a colonial con-

text, offering a first articulation of an "existential colonial angst" (Gorak, 69) and a vivid dramatization of "the effect of aggressive colonization on those who never chose to participate in the colonial process" (Gorak, 70). Irene Gorak argues that "Schreiner shows that colonization has imported into Africa its own conflicts, its own anxieties, its own inner darkness" (Gorak, 71). Thus *The Story of an African Farm* is located at "the fountainhead of much Third-World and Commonwealth literature" (Monsman 1991, xi) and has become amenable to interlinked feminist and postcolonial readings.

This recent linkage of the colonial and female predicaments affords insights into Schreiner's life and writing and is considered in the critical discussions of the works offered in this study. It is impossible to understand Schreiner's writing, fiction or nonfiction, without understanding how her subjectivity was constructed within a patriarchal colonial society that was oppressive in terms of race and gender, where multiple forms of dispossession bred multiple forms of transgression, transference, and engagement. It is also clear that Schreiner could operate in that society only by appropriating a masculine mask at times, of which her early male pseudonym, Ralph Iron, was one example. Her varied artistic strategies, stories, and voices constitute an attempt, within the boundaries of fiction, at a temporary integration of all the possible selves called into being by a fractured and oppressive reality, in a country where "wars were common"[14] and aggressive factional self-interest ruled. This fractured subjectivity has been seen in recent psychoanalytic theory as crucial to sexuality and the unconscious and to the construction of feminine sexuality and identity.[15]

Olive Schreiner's writing constantly sought to dream into being a harmonious and Utopian vision while acknowledging a state of inevitable present suffering and permanently deferred fulfillment. In this she was faithful to the deep conditions of female sexuality, storytelling, and identity as well as to the frontier violence of the South African condition when "the man with the gun was always there" (Schreiner, "Dawn," 913). Writing was her way of making space for an alternative voice to be heard, the voice of individual human rights, female equality, pacifism, and peaceful community. However, the racial conflict of the particular colony within which she grew up gave her narratives an ambiguous cast, as has recently been argued by Anne McClintock, who proposes that Schreiner's "mystical monism assuaged her loneliness and sense of exile, but was at odds with the social history of racial and gender difference that shaped her experience. . . . The most troubling presence of these imbalances appears in her work in the racial doubling of the mother figure."[16] This ambiguity has been seen as endemic to South African history and to its literature, in which a "discourse of race" has always encoded "appropriation and renunciation, aggression and resistance."[17] Although Schreiner's mystical monism may suggest a redemption anchored in South African landscape, her fiction constantly encodes the actualities of displacement and disappointment.

In the following analysis, Schreiner's fiction and nonfiction are regarded as complementary aspects of the same developing mind and art. Her formative experiences are presented within the context of white colonial English-speaking womanhood, a condition experienced as marginality and deferral, in which life and writing, South Africa and Europe, creativity and despair, alternated and often competed. Yet these conditions created the terms for Schreiner's responses—within the modes of fantasy, polemic, and narrative—to forms of powerlessness that she understood because she experienced many of them from the inside. The eloquence of language and self-expression became her bulwark and her public platform against social injustice, which she observed and interpreted not only in a South African context but also within the matrix of British imperialism.

I should like to thank the many people who have collaborated with me over the years and supported my research in various ways: Stephen Gray for his enthusiasm about my Schreiner projects and research in South African literature in general; Tony Voss for his unfailing encouragement, practical assistance, intellectual stimulus, and kindness while I was pursuing doctoral research and in every subsequent Schreiner paper or publication; Gillian Cargill for her enthusiasm and collaboration in fieldwork and Schreiner photography; Olive Renier for the donation of valuable manuscripts; Karel Schoeman for his meticulous biographical and literary research and assistance; Itala Vivan for her conference organization, translations, and publications concerning Schreiner; Joyce Berkman for her scholarly insights, friendship, and enthusiasm; Margaret Cartwright of the South African Library for her kind help when I was starting out on Schreiner research; the librarians at the special Schreiner collections in the libraries mentioned in the bibliography, within South Africa and elsewhere. I should also like to thank the Human Sciences Research Council of South Africa and the Research Office at the University of Guelph, Ontario, for making funds available to me for different phases and aspects of this research.

Chronology

1806	England takes the Cape Colony from the Dutch for the second time.
1834–1838	British Parliament emancipates slaves.
1836	The "Great Trek" begins; approximately five thousand Boer farmers leave the Cape and trek northward to protest slave emancipation and British "interference."
1838	Gottlob Schreiner and Rebecca Lyndall Schreiner, Olive Schreiner's parents, arrive as missionaries and work on the eastern frontier of the Cape Colony for the London Missionary Society. Their first child, Katharine Whitby Schreiner, born in the same year. The Boers defeat the Zulus at the Battle of Blood River.
1840	Frederick Samuel Schreiner born (he departed for school in England in 1853; he would later assist Olive in England).
1842	Albert Schreiner born (died March 1843).
1844	Theophilus Lyndall Schreiner born, later Temperance worker and member of the Legislative Assembly, then senator after the formation of the Union of South Africa.
1845	Alice Elizabeth Schreiner born, later Mrs. Hemming.
1848	Oliver Schreiner born.
1850	Henrietta Rebecca Schreiner born, later Temperance worker (became Mrs. Stakesby-Lewis).
1852	Emile Schreiner born. South African Republic (Transvaal) recognized as a republic.

1854	Oliver and Emile Schreiner die in Bloemfontein. Orange Free State recognized as a republic.
1855	Olive Emily Albertina Schreiner born on 24 March at Wittebergen Mission Station, Basutoland, named after her three dead brothers.
1857	William Philip Schreiner born, later Attorney-General to Rhodes, Prime Minister of the Cape from 1898–1900 and High Commissioner for South Africa in London from 1914 to his death in 1919.
1859	Cameron Schreiner born (dies in 1860).
1864	Helen Schreiner (Ellie) born (dies in 1865). *From Man to Man* was dedicated to Ellie.
1866	Gottlob Schreiner declared bankrupt after leaving missionary work and taking up local trading.
1867	Olive goes to Cradock to live with her elder brother and sister, Theo and Ettie, and her younger brother, Will. Diamond mining begins in Griqualand West.
1871	Olive changes her name from Emily and begins her life as companion/governess. Asthma attacks begin.
1872	Olive is briefly engaged to Julius Gau. Short stories more seriously written from this time on.
1873	First mention of *Undine Bock,* her first novel, posthumously published as *Undine.*
1875–1880	Working on two novels, one called *Saints and Sinners,* later published as *From Man to Man;* another, called *Lyndall* at one point, would become *The Story of an African Farm.*
1877	Britain annexes the Transvaal; Afrikaner Bond formed under Jan Hofmeyr.
1880	*African Farm* is evaluated by an Edinburgh publisher.
1880–1881	First Boer War, after which the Boers regain independence of Transvaal.
1881	Olive leaves for England to train as a nurse at Edinburgh Infirmary but becomes ill after a few days there. She submits her novels to publishers.

1883	*The Story of an African Farm* published in England by Chapman and Hall.
1884	Meets Havelock Ellis and Edward Carpenter. Begins intimate friendship with Ellis.
1885–1886	Involvement in Men and Women's Club and relationship with Karl Pearson.
1886	Gold mining begins on the Witwatersrand.
1887–1889	Traveling in Europe, working on allegories and *From Man to Man,* and planning preface to Wollstonecraft's *A Vindication of the Rights of Woman.* Becomes interested in Rhodes's grand schemes for Africa.
1889	Returns to South Africa.
1890	Meets Cecil Rhodes. Settles in Matjesfontein in the Karoo and begins her essays on South Africa.
1891	*Dreams* published.
1892	Meets Samuel Cron Cronwright, a farmer with political and literary interests.
1894	Marries Cronwright on 24 February. They abandon his Cradock farm for Kimberley because of her asthma.
1895	Birth and death of her baby girl, 30 April. Cron reads their paper, "The Political Situation," in the Kimberley Town Hall.
1896	Jameson Raid forces Rhodes to resign as Prime Minister of the Cape. Olive writes *Trooper Peter Halket of Mashonaland* and travels to England with Cron and the manuscript. *The Political Situation* published under their joint authorship.
1897	*Trooper Peter Halket* published in England.
1898	Olive goes to Johannesburg for her health; Cron follows her.
1899	Anglo-Boer War breaks out in November. *An English–South African's View of the Situation* published. The Schreiner house looted in Johannesburg.
1900	Living under martial law in Hanover, the Karoo.

	Writing war stories during these years; "Eighteen-Ninety-Nine" later published in *Stories, Dreams and Allegories*.
1902	Britain conquers the Afrikaner republics. Peace treaty signed.
1906–1907	*A Letter on the Jew* published. Britain gives parliamentary government to the former republics; only Whites enfranchised.
1908	Becomes one of the vice presidents of the Women's Enfranchisement League but resigns when it becomes clear that Black women were being excluded from the struggle for suffrage.
1909	*Closer Union* published, her views advocating federation in South Africa.
	Olive Schreiner's Thoughts about Women published for the Cape Women's Enfranchisement League (extracts from *African Farm* and *Dreams*). W. P. Schreiner and Gandhi lead protest delegation to London against Colour Bar in South Africa Bill.
1910	Cape Colony, Natal, Transvaal, and the Orange Free State formed into Union of South Africa, a white-controlled, self-governing British dominion under Louis Botha.
1911	*Woman and Labour* published.
1912	Founding of South African Native National Congress (NNC); later becomes the African National Congress (ANC).
1913	Leaves South Africa for England to seek remedies for heart problems, the same year the Native Land Act limits African land ownership to "reserves"; beginning of a series of segregation laws.
1914–1918	Britain declares war on Germany; South Africa participates in World War I.
1916	Writes for the *Labour Leader* in support of conscientious objectors to the war.
1919	Returns to South Africa, having given Cron her article "The Dawn of Civilization: Stray Thoughts

on Peace and War. The Homely Personal Confessions of a Believer in Human Unity." Published in *The Nation and the Athenaeum* in 1921.

1920	Dies during the night of 10 December in Wynberg, Cape Town.
1921	Reinterred with ceremony at top of Buffelskop, above Cron's old farm and Klein Gannahoek, where she wrote parts of *The Story of an African Farm* as a young governess.
	Communist Party of South Africa founded.
1923	*Thoughts on South Africa* and *Stories, Dreams, and Allegories* published.
1926	*From Man to Man* published.
1928	*Undine* published.
1948	The Afrikaner National Party wins a general election and begins to apply its policy of apartheid.
1955	The Congress of the People adopts a Freedom Charter.
1961	South Africa becomes a republic and leaves the British Commonwealth.
1994	The ANC wins the first nonracial election (April).
	Nelson Mandela sworn in as president (May 10) and forms the Government of National Unity. South Africa rejoins the British Commonwealth.

Chapter One

Shadows from Child-Life

Childhood: The Lost Joy

Childhood plays a crucial role in Olive Schreiner's life and writing. The adventures and landscapes of her youth, the strong nonconformist personalities and forces within her family, her early attachments and habits—all exerted a powerful influence on her personality and imagination, and to a certain extent held the adult woman in thrall. At the heart of her works are the intense and often lonely experiences of childhood, which provide the material for her most vivid scenes and narratives, such as the early chapters of *The Story of an African Farm* and the prelude to her unfinished novel, *From Man to Man*. She returned again and again to her childhood memories, revisited the places where she had grown up, and recalled the fierce pains and pleasures of her youth. Thus armed with a more objective, analytical point of view as an adult, Schreiner reexamined the spiritual crises, the experience of adult harshness, and the delight in nature she had herself known as a child.

Olive Emily Albertina Schreiner was the ninth child of Gottlob Schreiner and Rebecca Lyndall, who had arrived in South Africa in 1838 as missionaries for the London Missionary Society and who had settled at first on the eastern frontier that "lay across the route of the Great Trek, the large-scale exodus of Boer farmers from British colonial control that year" (First, 31). Gottlob and Rebecca never lost their sense of participation in a civilizing and Christianizing mission, and although Olive and her younger brother W. P. (Will) Schreiner later espoused the cause of the African people, Olive often spoke and wrote as a liberal member of a civilizing elite.

Olive was born at Wittebergen, an isolated Wesleyan mission station in what was then a native reserve on the edge of Basutoland (later Lesotho). The rocky grandeur and elevation of the mission house and chapel was a setting she would recapture in her chosen burial site, Buffelskop mountain in the Cradock area of the Cape Province. These mountain surroundings for birth and death reveal something about the self-conscious, even grandiose, lifestyle she pursued; they also shaped

1

her position as a pioneer possessed of controversial and even visionary ideas. She was aware of her own special imaginative ability, her writer's talent, and her idealistic intelligence, in that they could be both a blessing and a curse. Her earliest journal entry concerned the power of great thinkers, which she saw as grounded "in hours of solitude and silence."[1] She herself always found her deepest happiness alone in nature and did not cope well with complex social relations or the prolonged pressure of cities and people. Nevertheless, she used her solitary meditations to reflect deeply on social problems, political situations, the nature of experience, and, in particular, the problematic situation of women under Victorian patriarchy and in the crisis of modernity.

Schreiner felt that the circumstances of her birth linked her with her mother in a special way, through the earlier deaths of her three brothers, after whom she was named (she was called "Em" as a child but chose her first name, Olive, as a young girl, a first sign of her assuming a writer's mask). She recalls her early bond with her mother and her own inclination for storytelling:

> My mother never cared for her children especially her daughters as soon as they were older, say eight or nine. But of her tiny babies she was passionately fond. She was almost distracted when the little one died three months before my birth, and said she found no comfort in anything but walking up and down by herself behind the church which stood near the little mission house in which I was born. It's curious, as all my life since I was almost a baby of two or three, I've always had such a passion for walking up and down. One of the first things I can remember, when I can't have been more than three, was walking up and down in a passage with cocoanut [sic] matting on the floor and making stories to myself: and I can remember the other children laughing at me and my mother telling them they were to leave me alone.[2]

These habits of walking up and down and "making stories" would be lifelong and conditioned the strong rhythms and vivid scene painting of Schreiner's fiction, as did her mother's habit of having the children read the classics aloud. The circumstances of Schreiner's birth also indicate the ambiguity of her feelings for her mother, whom she admired as a brilliant, intellectual woman and a powerful personality, which she was. Schreiner compared her mother's face, when near death, to Cardinal Newman's (SCCS, *Letters,* 338). She was also, in Schreiner's view, less tenderhearted than their father: "[A]s children grow up," she concluded, always generalizing from her own family experience, "it is continually the father who gives the widest, most sympathetic love" (SCCS, *Letters*, 307), whereas mother love is instinctive and passes as her children grow into maturity. Schreiner's own responses to women were fluctuating and ambivalent: Her deepest friendships were with women, but she was often dubious of other women, suspecting them of sly manipulations of men and blaming them for male behavior. Her fiction and letters reveal her dislike of trivial, gossiping, fashionable women. Her novels always contain a portrait of a sly, manipulative, gossiping woman, one who is often successful with men but destructive in her relationships with other women. At certain points in her life Schreiner felt hounded by women and asserted that it was "awful to be a woman." She contended that "I've not been a woman really, though I've seemed like one" (SCCS, *Letters*, 142). Her marked ambivalence toward other women was thus bound up with her own self-ambivalence, with her perception that "to be born a woman is to be born branded"[3] and to be destined for fulfillment—if at all—only in the domestic sphere. She saw her mother's intellectual talents wasted by constant childbirth, the social isolation of mission stations, and a grinding poverty brought on by following her husband's failing fortunes in South Africa. It is no surprise that young talented women of the time associated womanhood with powerlessness and dependency when they contemplated the lives of their own mothers. Women endured all the disadvantages of second-rate citizens destined only for marriage, motherhood, and gentility (if they were white and middle class). One of Schreiner's key insights as a feminist was that women constituted a subordinate class in Victorian society, despite class differences among women. Schreiner's intense oscillations of self-image seem to go beyond such sociological causes, however, and carry the burden of the split self-image that, it has been argued, is the legacy of a patriarchal society. She appears to validate the arguments of feminist psychoanalytical critics who contend that the ego boundaries of women are more diffuse than those of men, who experience a more decisive ego formation and separation from infantile attachment to the mother.[4]

Schreiner's early responses to womanhood and sexuality were complicated by the fact that her mother punished her twice as a child with extremely harsh physical beatings for minor transgressions. This affected her sense of self-worth, lit a flame of outrage against any injustice, fueled by childish impotence and anger, and may have been a lifelong factor in her difficulties in forming continuously trusting relationships with others. To alter her self-destructive image of women, she needed positive relationships with other women. In one early letter she writes that her friend Mrs. Cawood is "quite converting my woman hatred into woman love" (Rive, *Letters*, 18–19). This core of pain around her sense of womanhood was one of the motives behind her lifelong campaign against injustices to women; it also deepened her intellectual formulations of the position of women and other marginalized or oppressed groups in society. Her mother's punishments—for offenses against English decorum and language—arose from a fear of contamination by the indigenous culture. Later Schreiner would passionately espouse the Boer cause during the Anglo-Boer War (1899–1902) and alienate her mother and older siblings, proving her loyalties as a first-generation South African.

Olive's father, Gottlob, a gentle, strong, dreamy, and impractical man, thus became a succoring figure for her. She saw her father and his Swabian forebears as peasant dreamers and rooted her character Waldo, in *The Story of an African Farm*, in this tradition. When she cast herself as a "dreamer" in the late 1880s, while writing her allegories, she was turning to her father's German philosophical traditions and recasting his dreams in a feminine Symbolist mode.[5] Her lifelong attachment to men, furthermore, and her heterosexual commitment to the ideal of monogamous marriage was very strong: "I believe there is, deep in human nature, a need for this close unending relationship with one above all who shall be as it were a part of oneself which it is the highest function of marriage to satisfy" (SCCS, *Letters*, 247). This lifelong need coexisted with the growing perception that marriage, for most women, meant the death of "her broad intellectual life as a free human creature."[6] Schreiner's unsullied love for her father, and his early death in 1876 when she was a young governess of 21, may have made her seek an impossible savior figure in any lover (her heroine Lyndall seeks "someone to worship"),[7] whereas her experience of her mother's beatings had attached love to pain and self-mistrust. Whatever the complex causes, any loss of a hoped-for union with a man was experienced as a repetition of her father's death, as a total abandonment. She sometimes seemed to seek out these experiences, wanting to see her first lover, Julius Gau, disembark in England or longing to see Karl Pearson after her relationship with him had ended: "I spent all the last days in the rain before University College hoping to catch a glimpse of him as he passed. I felt so when my father died" (SCCS, *Letters*, 71; Rive, *Letters*, 146). Scenes of parting and loss appear to be the most intensely felt aspects of a relationship and to condition the closure of her narratives. In such scenarios the pain of a lost lover could be renewed and confirm her sense that lovers were people who left, betrayed, or excluded you from their happy associations with other women.

At the same time, this principle of love renounced or lost was convenient in that it gave her the freedom to write, which could be achieved only outside marriage. Although she wanted a child, she "couldn't bear to be married," she wrote in 1886 (SCCS, *Letters,* 98). In spite of this, she would later marry and, despite the first years of companionship and happy affection, find that her experience confirmed her earlier fears, leaving her bitter once more about women's fate (SCCS, *Letters,* 281). It is difficult to know to what extent early fears acted as self-fulfilling prophesies. Scenes from *African Farm* reveal the importance of Olive's father as an emotional anchor; his early death allowed her to idealize his memory and to write tenderly about paternal affection in *African Farm,* whereas mother figures are absent or punitive.[8] Her father was a beacon of tender and protective affection that continued to lead her into new relationships with men. Although childhood was often "bitter and dark" because of restrictions on her freedom and family conflicts over religion, Schreiner nevertheless found solace in the rich physical environment: "[I]t was in nature I found all the joy and help I had in those lonely years" (SCCS, *Letters,* 266).

Associated with her earliest experience of being a living part of a greater whole, nature resonates throughout Schreiner's writing: "When I was a little child of five and sat alone among the tall weeds at the back of our house, this perception of the unity of all things, and that they were alive, and that I was a part of them, was as clear and overpowering as it is today" (Rive, *Letters,* 212). Her responses to the landscape were intense: The terrain of the mission stations of her childhood, especially Wittebergen and Healdtown, provided the imagery of an Eden that she re-created in her fiction; interestingly, a human snake of some kind often puts in an appearance in these idyllic settings. Nature—as a good and free place—is often contrasted with society, which is borne out by the historical associations of certain natural features: tree, kloof (wooded ravine), dam, or riverbed, close to each of the places where she lived in South Africa. These were private spots where she could walk about uninhibited and compose stories in peace. The method by which Schreiner creates this personal oasis is exemplified in the description of the little girl Rebekah, in the prelude to *From Man to Man,* on a hot Sunday afternoon on the farm:

> Rebekah followed a little winding footpath among the grass to the middle of the orchard, where a large pear tree stood with a gnarled and knotted stem. There was a bench under the tree, and the grass grew very long about it. She looked around to find a spot where the tree cast a deeper

shade than elsewhere. Here she walked round and round on the grass, like a dog, and then lay down on her back in the place she had made. It was like a nest, with the grass standing several inches high all round.[9]

Nature offered an alternative home; the Karoo landscape especially—in which she would later be a governess and write or revise her early fiction—delighted her by the freedom it offered. Both the microscopic creatures dwelling in the red sand and the Karoo's vast perspectives seemed to have predated human suffering. Each component of the surroundings had both an individuality and a connection to the larger, harmonious structure:

> Do you know the effect of this scenery is to make me so silent and self-contained. And it is so bare—the rocks and the bushes, each bush standing separate from the others alone by itself. I went (on) a long walk this morning away out into the Karoo and found some large bent old trees in the dry river course. I will make that my walking up and down place. I like very much being so free—it is like having a house of your own without the trouble of taking care of it. (Rive, *Letters,* 168)

This combination of individuality and belonging, a coherent organic pattern, was a physical embodiment of her own sense of what a work of art should be, what she felt her own novels attempted to be, as well as a metaphor for her ideal human community or social structure. Her childhood experience predisposed her to value the principle of a free organic unfolding of potential very highly; as a result, her writing becomes protest fiction because, in women, that free unfolding was usually constrained from the start by discriminatory educational practices and gender stereotypes. Schreiner's fictional little girls are often forbidden to romp or play freely; little girls especially had to protect their complexion, and she herself was expected to follow a certain decorum dictated by her mother's standards of middle-class English refinement. Her fictional children—like Undine, in Schreiner's first novel, who goes off in wild pursuit of her pet monkey—take immense delight in places and activities that allow physical energy and pleasure. As a young woman, Olive enjoyed rolling down the mine dumps at New Rush (later Kimberley). Victorian social constraints cut in upon women in many ways, and another of these was dress. Schreiner refused to wear the obligatory corsets, had very few clothes—none of them fashionable—and was therefore laughed at by indigenous South African women as she walked down Government Avenue. She tried to protest the social conformity expected of women and sometimes met ridicule as a result.

One of the formative events of Olive's childhood was the death of her younger sister Ellie (Helen) at 18 months, when Schreiner was 10 years old. Her love for Ellie, her only younger sister, spawned a protective love of other women that is developed in *From Man to Man*. Nurturing feelings were aroused by her sister's birth, and her "love for women and girls, not because they are myself, but because they are not myself, comes from my love to her" (SCCS, *Letters,* 274). She speaks about her female characters in the same way, emphasizing similarity and difference, or distance. Clearly, her relationship with Ellie was important for the development of a more discrete female self, one who could mother as well as be mothered. The psychological process is creatively represented in Schreiner's prelude to *From Man to Man,* in which feelings of sibling envy and rivalry are overcome and in which a fantasized mothering and storytelling are crucial. The prelude thus provides a link between female bonding and storytelling, especially to a more vulnerable female with whom the narrator identifies. Storytelling served a healing and integrative function for Schreiner. She had to accept Ellie's death while trying to resolve her difficulties with the Calvinist view of the afterlife, sin, damnation, and predestination. Ellie's death proved pivotal in Schreiner's denial of Christian dogma. Her acceptance of Ellie's death after sleeping next to her dead body and keeping a vigil at her grave changed her view of the finality of death and "made a freethinker of me" (SCCS, *Letters,* 274). Ellie's death taught her the falsity of her earlier beliefs and made "all life" a miracle " because it had brought forth and taken back to itself such a beautiful thing as she was to me" (Rive, *Letters,* 213). Olive identified with her own mother's bereavements ; she became, briefly, a mother herself. These feelings are portrayed in Rebekah's anxious concerns for her sister Bertie and the predicted reunion of the sisters at Bertie's death, in *From Man to Man*. Bonding between women, female creativity and storytelling, jealousy and protective affection, are crucial in Schreiner's fictions and shape the patterns of her narratives. Other women are always both ourselves and not ourselves.

Olive's experience of the death of a sibling seems to have outranked in her imagination her relationships with her living sisters and brothers, except her younger brother Will. She had little in common with two of her elder sisters, Kate and Alice, who both married and had large families; Alice died young, and her surviving children were taken in by Ettie (Henrietta), the kindhearted but apparently credulous older sister who became a committed temperance worker and later a source of great comfort to the poor and the outcast of Cape Town. Fred, Olive's eldest brother, had left to attend school in England before she was born, although she had an affectionate relationship with him when she was in England and called him her "dadda." Fred was a respectable school principal and founder of New College, Eastbourne, in Sussex, and cut his ties with Olive for a while when *African Farm* caused a scandal among the bourgeoisie. Theo, also an older brother, had been a kind friend when Olive was young, but became the persecutor of her adolescence when she dared to question Christianity. Olive's closest emotional tie and intellectual kinship was with her younger brother, Will, a generous and brilliant man who was briefly Prime Minister of the Cape Colony and later South African High Commissioner in London. The four leading Schreiners—Theo, Ettie, Will and Olive—became a force to be contended with in Cape liberal politics, although they often pulled in different directions. Ettie's early independence and her public role as an impassioned public speaker on temperance issues influenced Olive when she was young and demonstrated how a degree of public activity and influence was possible for women.

The relationship between Ettie and Olive illustrates how feminist protest grew historically out of the evangelical tradition and the temperance movement. Feminist historian Jane Rendall argues that the legacy of evangelical belief offered a "re-evaluation of women's domestic and moral status" and had "both conservative and radical possibilities for the situation of women."[10] Ettie and Olive represent those different possibilities in a colonial context. The evangelical context of Olive's youth had constraining and damaging effects as well, with its emphasis on selflessness, sin, "the breaking of the will and the denial of self" (Rendall, 73). Olive's mother used these terms in relation to parenting and submission to God's will. Parents were seen as surrogates of divine authority over the child; a husband's authority over his wife also had divine sanction in this pattern of analogous hierarchies. When—between the ages of 9 and 14—Olive wrestled with the issue of faith and free thought, she was attempting to throw off many types of restrictive authority, with far-reaching effects. At that time her elder brother Theo and her sister Ettie were keeping house together and thus acting as surrogate parents, which complicated her responses to their disapproval and led to a degree of persecution. This claustrophobic atmosphere permeates Schreiner's first novel, *Undine*. The evangelical ideal of obedient selflessness helps to explain Olive's own sense of "wickedness" and the difficulty she had in claiming pleasure and fulfillment for herself. It also explains her lifelong struggle between a sense of duty to her talent and writing and the duty she felt she owed to the human community. Her youthful dream of becoming a doctor was satisfying because medicine combined knowledge with service to humanity. She often allowed her energy to be claimed by urgent social and political issues rather than by the writing of fiction, which could be seen as decidedly self-interested. The writing of her "big novel," *From Man to Man,* was related to her idea that the novel would help other women by revealing that they did not suffer alone. It was harder for her to admit that writing had something to do with the ego, ambition, and a desire for immortality, which she felt compelled to renounce. Such "temptations" are also rejected by the quester in her Hunter allegory in *African Farm.*[11] Probably the most significant spiritual aspect of Schreiner's youth was her own religious crisis, which had a pronounced effect on the fictional scenes she crafted of young people struggling with faith, science, and disbelief. Her first two novels portrayed two aspects of that struggle, the first mainly concerned with the everyday social hypocrisy of Christians, in *Undine,* and the second with the phases of a spiritual crisis brought about by the rejection of God. Undine and Waldo are terrified by a vision of souls going to hell; Waldo suffers intensely as he loses his sense of being embraced by the love of God; Lyndall's deathbed vision is of a world redeemed by suffering. Spiritual answers could also be found in Emerson's essay "Self-Reliance" or in John Stuart Mill's rational humanism. Typically, however, Schreiner's characters experience a spiritual illumination of place and time in moments of solitude within an African landscape. When Olive began her reading of "physical science," she said that the "agonizing disorganization" of her spiritual life ended, and religion became "one unending joy," a sense that "God" was a loving and creative principle diffused throughout creation (Rive, *Letters,* 213–14).

In her youthful journals we see the everyday struggles of an isolated colonial girl trying to come to terms with a worldview apparently split in two by her rejection of organized religion. We see her dissecting small creatures, studying science and medicine, and searching for answers in her reading, her reflections, and her intense, mystical responses to African landscapes: "The bush was like her home."[12] Childhood involved painful doubts about the world and her relationship with it; at the same time it also seemed to provide the means of overcoming those doubts: "And so, it comes to pass in time, that the earth ceases for us to be a weltering chaos. . . . the sky . . . raises itself into an immeasurable blue arch over our heads, and we begin to live again" (*SAF,* 143). This process of conflict and difficult resolution is the direction in which she takes her fictional characters: They often find themselves alone in moments of crisis, and the solutions they find are difficult inner answers involving the whole being. Childhood's intense suffering and the responses it evoked became—for Olive Schreiner—the foundation of adult life and human identity.

Julius Gau: Seduction and Betrayal

If Schreiner's religious crisis forms one axis of her fictional world, her radical critique of social conventions as they affected the women of her day forms the other. Many of her views on female education, freedom of movement, pacifism, sexuality, and marriage took years to formulate, but certain experiences in her adolescence sharpened her sense of female vulnerability and showed her what the process of courtship and marriage actually meant for a girl like herself. She learned that social conventions are not necessarily congruent with human desires or with emotional honesty. In particular, the gap that existed between sexual behavior and public morality cropped up in both her life and her fiction. A pivotal experience was her first love affair, at the age of 17, with a businessman, Julius Gau. Her fictional accounts of sexual unconventionality, difficulties in courtship, and a sense of fundamental damage and exposure all draw on the complex sense of shame, sinfulness, and social exposure, which such a bold relationship in a small South African village, Dordrecht, was bound to cause. The memory of this relationship haunted her adult years, and insignificant incidents much later in life stirred up a "hidden agony" associated with the public exposure of and gossip about her private sexual behavior (Rive, *Letters,* 151–52). This nightmarish sense of exposure demonstrates how radical an act it was to give oneself sexually to a man outside marriage at the time and how self-righteously and punitively society treated women who did so. The line between respectable married women and prostitutes was clear: Although Olive tried to live outside such conventional beliefs, she had grown up inside them, and they were hard to cast aside completely. Her lifelong sense of "agonized oneness" with prostitutes and her attempts in England to help them and to theorize their role in Victorian society stems partly from her sense that she had behaved like one, at least in terms of Victorian public morality.[13]

Schreiner's relationship with Julius Gau, a conventional and ambitious young businessman in the village where she lived during her first informal governess posting, was intertwined with many other damaging pressures that had been building up in her life. Her father's bankruptcy in 1866 and the family's dire poverty had meant that Olive found herself homeless. She first stayed with her older brother and sister in Cradock, an arrangement that led to many conflicts; she then was sent to the family of the Reverend Zadoc Robinson to serve as both domestic help and governess to the children. During these years of financial difficulty, she was often in this loosely defined, dependent, and rather humiliating position. The restlessness and emotional anxiety she experienced in this period would recur throughout her life: "I am thoroughly sick of this life always having to move on and never knowing where to move on to" (Rive, *Letters,* 5). Marriage might have seemed to hold out some promise of security and affection, but she had not learned that virginity was the bargaining power behind middle-class marriage and that an upwardly mobile young businessman (Gau worked for an insurance firm) did not marry a penniless young woman who had "put herself into (his) power, and who [had] lost the right of meeting (him) on equal terms" (*SAF,* 222). The Gau affair led to a real or suspected pregnancy, a quick engagement, and a long, arduous coach journey to her parents in the small village of Hertzog. This was the prototype for many such ill-fated coach journeys during this period and for the almost surreal and fragmented journey Lyndall undertakes with her stranger in *African Farm,* which ends in her death.[14] The possible pregnancy and miscarriage (or abortion) that followed probably also accounts for the dead babies that haunt her fiction. Shortly after the public announcement of their engagement, the betrothal was broken by Gau, who must have been horrified by her parents' penury as well as increasingly alienated by his fiancée's unconventional views. This abrupt ending, which was followed by a brief period of depression and gloom, was a shock for Olive.

The effects of this relationship—one of which was Olive's determination that her books would be her only children—were extremely long-term psychologically. She would always be affected by gossip, and her sensitivity to being discussed by others (perhaps an unfortunate quality in a woman whose views were often controversial) at times led to panic-stricken flight. Her fiction would concern itself primarily with the plight of the innocent girl ruined (*Wrecked* is an early manuscript title) by the contradictions of sexual morality, the double standard of behavior for men and women, the economic nature of the marriage contract, and the unequal manner in which men and women were socialized, educated, and married. She had trustingly and naively assumed that there could be love, friendship, and desire in one relationship with a man and that marriage might simply be the final seal on this organic development. She may have also assumed that freedom of opinion for women could coexist with marriage. What her fiction and her letters tell us—and what Schreiner's feminist study would later confirm—was that none of these assumptions was fact. Young women had to assume subservient roles in all these processes and submit to male authority, social decorum, and economic dependence. Schreiner would spend her life working out the implications of these experiences and reworking them in her fiction. But her instincts about their injustice were sound.

After marriage had become a mirage, the question of where she would go and what she would do was crucial. Her attempts at self-education were courageous, but books could offer only so much help and were often a stimulus to her thoughts, an emotional consolation, or a spiritual guide. She returned home briefly, then joined Theo and Ettie at New Rush, where the bustling atmosphere of the diamond diggings reenergized her and stimulated her desire to capture some of these animated scenes on paper. However, she would have to earn her own living, after her vain hope that a large diamond would enable her to go abroad for a proper education came to nothing. On another long, disastrous coach trip, her portmanteau containing all her belongings was stolen. Without resources, connections, food, or money, Olive was not gladly received at home, where her mother's poverty had soured any welcome for such an improvident and careless daughter. At this juncture, Olive developed asthma, clearly evincing the distress caused by her sense of suffocation at home, lack of prospects away from home, rage, disappointment, and helplessness. Over time, her asthma had serious effects on her lungs, heart, and general well-being. Such physiological manifestations might be considered a vivid metaphor of the unbreachable impasse between self and society, sexuality and decorum, family and lovers, which many nineteenth century women endured in silence. Schreiner would live out her life as a restless, driven woman with very few periods of stability. Writing became her only respite.

The Little Governess

Schreiner would be employed as a governess between 1874 and early 1880 (she left South Africa for England early in 1881). These years were most fruitful ones in terms of her fiction, as she completed almost three of her four novels. She also discovered the disadvantages of being an underpaid and exploited laborer at certain points, although on the whole she seems to have enjoyed teaching children, perhaps because her own education had been hard won. Her knack for devising simple and vivid analogies, as her explanatory or polemical prose shows, must have stood her in good stead as a teacher. She often writes in her journal of her pupils' progress, and she had clearly won their affection (apart from one large Boer girl who attacked her with a slate). Her first, more formal, posting was with an English-speaking family named Weakley, in Colesberg. Mr. Weakley was a newspaper owner and shopkeeper, and Olive was employed as a shop assistant, proofreader, domestic help and general baby-sitter, seamstress, and governess. She would fall asleep in her clothes from exhaustion and drew upon these experiences as the basis of her portrait of Waldo's work in *African Farm*. She was also sexually exploited by, or at least sexually vulnerable to, her employer, as she had been with Zadoc Robinson. She seems to have been drawn into a form of romantic or physical intimacy that she would have been powerless to resist except by leaving. Emotionally needy at the time, she must have been susceptible to the appeal of an older, apparently caring, man. Also, her refusal to teach religious instruction always played a role in these tutoring situations, affecting both what she was paid and the family's attitude toward her. It was often the ostensible reason given for her dismissal, whereas she was usually the one who became dissatisfied and desperately sought another situation. Her presence under these conditions would have become a trigger for jealousy as well as moral disapproval.

The other families for whom Schreiner worked as a governess were Boer families, and she retained a special affection for and a protective interest in "the Boer," as her later articles for English journals indicated. The cultural differences were often entertaining, although Schreiner participated in some of her mother's patronizing and superior attitudes inherited from British imperialism; her Boer characters are stereotypically gross and less refined than her English heroines. Nevertheless, she gained a closer knowledge of Boer life and customs, of the deep religious faith that sustained the Great Trek and kept families together, of the often inhuman treatment of indigenous people who were classified as outside that faith and seen as a convenient labor pool, and of the suspicion of all literature outside the *Bible*. Her Tant Sannie in *African Farm* embodies the suspicion and conservatism of the upcountry Boer and becomes a foil for the new generation as well as an embodiment of a tenacious attachment to the land and a conservative religious tradition. The Fouchés, for whom Schreiner worked twice as a governess, provided anecdotes and a source of information and humor that served as the basis of some of the portraits of Boer life in her fiction and nonfiction. The Martin family was more refined and better educated, and the husband, previously a Dutch Reformed minister, was particularly congenial because he was a dissenter. While teaching at Gannahoek, the Fouchés' farm, Olive was also intimate with an English family, the Cawoods, who lived in a cottage nearby and who later became prosperous farmers in the area. She moved between these two families, gathering a comparative perspective on both cultures. She was creating characters and stories quite intensely, as these years gave time for reading, writing, friendship, and reflection after much turbulence and distress. A certain sifting of the troubled familial and sexual relationships of the previous years took place in her fiction. Her characters—Undine, Lyndall, Waldo, Em, Rebekah, and Bertie—could express the meaning of these experiences in a more distanced and impersonal, yet creatively liberating, way. Schreiner was also influenced by the teeming life of the area around her: the mimosa bushes, the red sand, ostriches, beetles, monkeys, koppies, and kraals, a sense of seething animal and plant life that always gave her the "will to live" (Rive, *Letters,* 216). The landscape itself could offer a bare and desolate prospect, mocking failed hopes and plans, or be transformed into an ethereal beauty by moonlight. Cultivated gardens shaded into wildflower patches in the bush, and then into scrub, sand and stunted bushes. Schreiner's deepest attachments and most profound peace were inextricably intertwined with African landscapes.

Although Schreiner's treatment of the indigenous people in her writing may seem complacent or patronizing, her position was that of an English-speaking Cape liberal. Her early views were an expression of "the universal language of European and American political liberalism" in conflict with a "slave-owning society."[15] Dr. John Philip, under whose aegis Schreiner's parents had traveled to Africa, would play a central role in slave emancipation. The British inhabitants of South Africa assumed a belief in their cultural and moral superiority to Boer views and habits, including the Boers' treatment of slaves and indigenous people. Nevertheless, Schreiner's own views evolved from her childish "fully developed Jingoism" to a more nuanced sympathy and "an increased knowledge."[16] Her sympathies were developed by her progressive understanding of the marginal position of women in colonial society, and she often uses African women as the mouthpiece of bitterness at women's plight, at least in her letters and anecdotes.[17] She realized that African women were much more fully the property of men than were white colonial women: "The Kaffir female is the property of the male; he may kill, flog or subject her to any use, owing to his superior physical strength; but her functions as builder, manufacturer, cultivator, prevent any deterioration of her mental powers and her physical strength ("MW," 10) Her view of the Khoi (Hottentot) or Kaffir (then the term for African, Nguni) men was significantly shaped by her sense that they often physically abused their women. In general, Schreiner's model was evolutionary, and she tends to see the indigenous people on lower rungs of the evolutionary hierarchy. At the time she was first writing, and in the Cape Colony that she knew, slavery was the issue, not the racial segregation that later came to be codified and rigidified in South Africa in the twentieth century. With slaves she had an instinctive empathy, identifying with runaways and protesting their brutal punishment for small offenses. The San people, too, figure sympathetically in *African Farm* as the painters of rock art. The center of compassion, however, is always the innocently victimized young colonial girl. As women were a marginalized and often silenced group, only writing—one of the few outlets for women—could give them an effective voice and make them a force to contend with in the public sphere, which was almost entirely the domain of men. Schreiner's volubility, despite her sometimes incomplete formal writing, served to protest against the conditions of women like her—everywhere. Schreiner's fiction focused on colonial relationships like the ones she had experienced so intimately as a young colonial woman. In her fiction she would represent and transform them, but by doing so with vividness and passion she would make her work speak for and to other women. Her novels found a deep resonance in many readers.

Writing the "Problem Novel"

Olive Schreiner's fiction can be seen as an index to the major changes affecting the relationship between individuals and society toward the end of the nineteenth century. She summarized those changes:

> [T]he substitution of mechanical for hand labour, the wide diffusion of knowledge through the always increasing cheap printing press; the rapidly increasing gathering of human beings into vast cities . . . ; the increasingly rapid means of locomotion; the increasing intercourse between distant races and lands, brought about by rapid means of intercommunication, widening and changing in every direction the human horizon—all these produce a society, so complex and so rapidly altering,

that social co-ordination between all its parts is impossible. Social unrest, and the strife of ideals, of faiths, of institutions, and consequent human suffering is inevitable. (*WL*, 265–66)

She argued that this diversity, caused by very different degrees of adaptation to complex and rapid changes in society, caused great friction and suffering, which "is only describable in the medium of art, where actual concrete individuals are shown acting and reacting on each other—as in the novel or drama" (*WL*, 268). This central topic is acted out in the lives of her characters. She suggested that this social conflict is found within individuals, in "struggle, conflict, and disco-ordination," and that "the man or woman who attempts to adapt their life to the new material conditions and to harmony with the new knowledge, is almost bound at some time to rupture the continuity of their own psychological existence" (*WL*, 270). These conditions affect the art of the age, which "tends persistently to deal with subtle social problems, religious, political and sexual, to which the art of the past holds no parallel." The artist must inevitably do this because he "must portray that which lies at the core of its life" (*WL*, 270). Thus the problem play, novel, or poem is an inevitable expression of the major social and cultural changes, rooted in material change, that make up the period. Schreiner clearly had her own writing, as well as that of George Eliot, Hardy, Ibsen, Meredith, and Dickens in mind when formulating these ideas in her maturity, in *Woman and Labour* (1911). What she herself adds to this portrayal of the sufferings of emergent modern men and women is the South African setting, a stress on the advanced intellectual as a tragic leader figure, and a linkage between imperialism and patriarchy. What is also characteristic of her representations of these "New Men and Women" is her constant emphasis on sexuality as the primary zone of dis-coordination because "when we enter the region of sex we touch, as it were, the spinal cord of human existence, its great nerve centre, where sensation is most acute, and pain and pleasure most keenly felt. It is not sex disco-ordination that is at the root of our social unrest; it is the universal disco-ordination which affects even the world of sex phenomena" (*WL*, 271). These ideas were a later summation of what Schreiner herself had lived through and compose the major focus of her novels.

Schreiner's other allegiance, as she wrote in her preface to *African Farm*, was to her local habitation and place, the "grey pigments" that lie all around the South African artist and that cannot be abandoned or distorted for the sake of melodrama. The artist tries to be faithful "to the scenes among which he has grown" (*SAF,* preface). She was a colonial Victorian woman who constantly used the masculine pronoun for the artist, as if the woman artist did not exist, and had to be called into being by writers like herself. Her rural isolation on South African farms had other effects on her art: She writes to Havelock Ellis about the didacticism that affects the solitary colonial writer (Rive, *Letters,* 35). As he pointed out, her colonialism was also the source of her strength, her personal syntax, and her style. She displays the integrity of someone who made her own discoveries and worked out her own principles for behavior and belief. Her reliance on the truth of her own vision, the idiosyncrasy of her syntax, and her often homely South African analogies reveal a writer far from the centers of literary sophistication but with a tough self-confidence in the value of her ideas and the craggy individuality of the artistic methods she used.

Schreiner's fiction was grounded in experience and the organic, instinctive ordering of that experience in narrative. The strengths of provincial art have been discussed by Kenneth Clark: a concern with facts, narrative, lyricism, and a visionary intensity.[18] Schreiner's distance from metropolitan centers encouraged the development of these qualities, which have become intertwined with her feminist and socialist protest. Her fiction arises at a point when Puritanism was dying and eternal verities, as well as social codes, were being called into question, including the British Empire, from which those values derived. Her novels reveal the loss of those verities and the sufferings of those who sought to make their lives meaningful in their absence—on the edges of the empire. Her fiction shows us a world of discordant human relationships as men and women seek reassurance from each other and the natural world. The answers, for Olive Schreiner, lay in the house of language and fiction.

Chapter Two

Father-Empire and Mother-Right: The Sexual Politics of Narrative

Olive Schreiner's works were forged in the crucible of Victorian imperialism and its concomitant patriarchy. They were also influenced by the subversive movements of the late nineteenth century that contested both these systems of domination. A strong movement aimed to redefine the situation of women and the working classes, resulting in a newly perceived mobility across gender categories that had hitherto been deemed absolute. As Elaine Showalter has argued, the late nineteenth century was a time when "myths, metaphors and images of sexual crisis"[1] proliferated; the boundaries of masculinity and femininity became mutable, and the roles of women no longer seemed so easily determined or satisfactory. Marriage as a property contract or a partnership of unequals was being condemned by writers such as Henrik Ibsen, Thomas Hardy, George Moore, and George Meredith, and by cultural pioneers such as Havelock Ellis and Edward Carpenter, two of Schreiner's closest friends in the London of the 1880s. The publication of *The Story of an African Farm* in 1883 was a crucial catalyst in the evolution of new types of community, individual sexual choices, and labor relations. In England, the book was received in a context of New Woman novels that reappraised realism and the ideology of "womanliness" in relation to the domestic sphere.[2]

Women's oppression was a powerful, emergent theme at this time; as Schreiner's friend Karl Pearson pointed out, the two great problems of modern social life were perceived as those of women and labor.[3] Although embedded in colonial forms of contemporary British reaction to race and class, Schreiner's writing also contributed to a deeper understanding of particular issues. These included women's relationships with one another, their social roles and sexuality, a "dialectic between womanhood and power" (Auerbach, 186) that she helped to construct and that made the writings of New Women a pioneering moment in the genealogy of modernism.[4] The struggles of powerless or marginal colonial subjects, especially women, against divisive, constricting, and arbitrary social codes of behavior would be the great theme of Schreiner's writings, both polemical and fictional. Her protest was personally sanctioned but influenced a wide audience of readers through the translation of key publications throughout Europe. As Showalter points out, *African Farm* "helped to establish the intellectual basis and the rhetorical tropes of turn of the century feminism," (p. 47) and *Woman and Labour* (1911) was one of the first efforts to link feminism and capitalism and to present the problems of modern women in a historicized, materialist framework. Schreiner's prose, in the words of Patricia Stubbs, has a "prophetic quasi-religious quality"; it "inspired, revealed and explained the women's movement to itself: grasping in her imagination the spirit and aims of the struggle, she welded them into an impassioned and eloquent whole."[5]

The ideological battle to subvert cultural stereotypes of women and cultural conventions concerning "male and female, romance and quest, hero and heroine, public and private" (Du Plessis, ix) was fought out in the novel, as Schreiner herself recognized: "[T]he novel has taken the place of other forms of art in carrying to the heart of the people the truths (or untruths) of the Age. . . . From the Queen to the servant girl and Smith and Sons news boys everyone reads the novel and is touched by it. Its vice and its virtue, its frivolity and its ideals, all the life of our age is incarnate in its fiction, and reacts on the people" (Rive, *Letters,* 109). Nancy Armstrong argues that "the history of the novel cannot be understood apart from the history of sexuality," that "written representations of the self allowed the modern individual to become an economic and psychological reality," and that the modern individual was first and foremost a woman.[6] Along with Ibsen, Hardy, Moore, and Meredith, Schreiner helped to construct a freer mode of sexual expression for women by revealing how the honesty and vulnerability of "pure women" led to crippling and disastrous consequences.[7] Schreiner's books exposed an array of contradictions and restrictions that confronted the women who inveighed against social convention, limited education for women, and unsubstantiated notions of romantic and domestic fulfillment. In Schreiner's often twinned protagonists, the relentlessly divided subjectivity of women under patriarchy is forcefully expressed as her heroines struggle between aspiration and despair, rebellion and conformity, romantic love and a desire for fulfilling, independent activity. Moreover, her protagonists' struggles were played out on the edges of the British Empire, thus linking abuses against women with "the abuses associated with British imperial expansion" (Monsman, xiii). Because

Schreiner's writing stands on the fulcrum of the British Empire and colony, her passionate social protest also exposed the nature of power inherent in colonization.

The struggles within Schreiner's fiction, like her own struggle for independence and creativity as an author, were partly a resistance to a closure of form that might also deny her a glimpsed but as yet unrealized harmony between herself and the world. After abandoning Christianity, she was especially dependent on the ideal of a future secular perfectibility. As Stubbs says of Hardy's fiction, there is a struggle "between available literary and sexual images and Hardy's efforts to portray real women, characters who are individualized and yet demonstrate convincingly women's predicament in society as a whole." (Stubbs, 83). Many readers have testified to the vitality and power of Schreiner's colonial heroines, whose struggles were—in the main—those of all nineteenth-century women who sought freedom from the tyranny of patriarchy, orthodox religion, and conventional marriage. However, Schreiner's portraits of white South African women reflect the face of the British Empire. Lyndall, Rebekah, and Bertie move through closely rendered South African landscapes: Karoo farms, veld, upcountry town, and Cape Town, pursuing the broken dreams of young women aspiring to love, freedom, and independent labor in unpromising colonial circumstances. In their yearning toward fulfillment, they constantly enmesh themselves further in the penalties meted out to nonconforming women, those who seek a space for growth outside conventional roles within the family. Even when they break through some of society's restraints, as Undine, the heroine of Schreiner's first completed novel, does, they find that many of these restrictions have been internalized, that "a woman is a poor thing carrying in herself the bands that bind her."[8] Schreiner's novels both contest and reaffirm the resilience of the "romantic love narrative": According to Rabine, romantic love "provides one of the few accepted outlets through which women can express their anger and their revolt against their situation in a patriarchal order but also idealizes and eroticizes women's powerlessness and lack of freedom."[9] This ambivalence colored Schreiner's writing and was an integral part of her life, representing a crucial inconsistency in Victorian women's books, "simultaneously subverting and conforming to patriarchal standards."[10] The impurity of female desires as they struggle for autonomy is an aspect of women's lives that Schreiner consciously and unconsciously reveals.[11]

In portraying the lives of these nineteenth-century colonial girls and women, Schreiner—an early and almost compulsive writer—was setting herself up against established Victorian authors, instinctively and artistically reworking genres and adapting conventions to suit the truths she wanted to convey. By attending to the margins in a new way, argues Ann Ardis, New Woman books like Schreiner's eroded the distinction between high and popular fiction and often liberated a female character's voice from the omniscient narrator's control. Thus they constructed a polyphonic discourse that called linear narratives, the "natural" inevitability of the marriage plot, and patriarchal history into question (Ardis, 3). The Victorian angel in the house is replaced by (or sometimes compared with) a heroine who is sexually active outside marriage, even though Schreiner's endings often reinstalled the principle of selfless love for women and thus could be read as validating the romance plot, in which the heroine's death "leaves the Victorian social order intact" (Miller cited by Ardis, 66). We have to read the heroine's aspirations and visions of emancipation against the grain of her actual defeat.

Some of these affiliations and distinctions are made clear in Schreiner's responses to the more extensive reading she was doing in London in the early eighties and discussing with Havelock Ellis or other friends. George Eliot was probably the most inescapable literary presence for any woman writer at the time, and Schreiner distinguished herself from Eliot by saying that "her great desire was to teach, mine to express myself, for myself and to myself alone. . . . If God were to put me alone on a star and say I and the star should be burnt up at last and nothing be left, I should make stories all the time just the same" (Rive, *Letters,* 154). Although this conveys the involuntary and expressive nature of Schreiner's writings and licenses interpretations that emphasize the links between her protagonists and her own experiences, it is also an oversimplification. Elsewhere she speaks of desired effects on particular audiences, of helping other women with her books, or satirizing and correcting attitudes, as she attempts to do in *Trooper Peter Halket of Mashonaland.* When Schreiner was writing her own novels in South Africa before 1881, she had read *The Mill on the Floss,* although she professed to like it in spite of her general antipathy to novel reading, preferring "science or poetry" (Rive, *Letters,* 286). In her letters she mentions *Adam Bede* (Rive, *Letters,* 49), and some of the peaceful impersonal rendering of rural lifestyles characteristic of Eliot is found in her chapter describing a Boer wedding in *African Farm.* Eliot died on December 29, 1880, two months before Schreiner arrived in England. Schreiner's oeuvre could be seen as a shattered colonial version of Eliot's eloquent and consistent creativity and achievement; contributing factors were Schreiner's fragmented self-education, her lifelong search for self-identity, and her struggle with childhood neuroses attributable to life within her strict evangelical family. Schreiner's marital relationship with S. C. Cronwright would be conceived much as was Eliot's relationship with G. H. Lewes: a novel-writing "genius" sheltered and nurtured by a caring partner. In Schreiner's case this expectation eventually caused much bitterness, when her row of anticipated masterpieces did not appear—or did not appear in time to be economically useful. This difficult financial situation, her gradually deteriorating marriage, and her inability to complete much creative work while she was married all attest to the way in which she perceived marriage and artistic work as mutually exclusive.

Schreiner's fiction has some affiliations with that of Dickens and the Brontës, the earlier "novels of 1848," in which "scenes of unjustified punishment generate tremendous outrage on behalf of the powerless" (Armstrong, 177). The anger and resentment of a powerless class in the works of Dickens and the Brontës is paralleled by the punitive scenes Schreiner constructs involving colonial children, such as Waldo's flogging in *African Farm* and the socially redemptive roles played by the deaths of such "children" who remain "little" even as adult women. She had read *Dombey and Son* (1848) in South Africa and was therefore familiar with a work that made childhood "the affective center of fiction and validating touchstone for human worth."[12] Evangelical tracts and the "exemplary piety of dying children" (Spilka, 174) underpin Little Nell of Dickens's *Old Curiosity Shop* (1841) as well as Harriet Beecher Stowe's Little Eva in *Uncle Tom's Cabin* (1852), which Schreiner read before leaving South Africa in 1881.[13] Her fiction, especially her story "Dream Life and Real Life" and *Trooper Peter Halket of Mashonaland* (1897), reveals strong affinities with abolitionist narratives. Orphans are the foils to adult corruption in *Undine* and *African Farm*, exposing cruelty, hypocrisy, and the punitive distortions of doctrines such as predestination, which were much discussed in the religious disputes of her family. Her children take Biblical texts, moral exhortations, and personal faith seriously, thus portraying by means of their purity an adult world that does not. In three of her four novels (although even in *Trooper Peter* there are flashbacks to earlier years), childhood provides a structural prelude to the main action, exerts a continuing force over adolescents and adults, and offers a controlling metaphor of purity of vision and endless potential, a potential crushed by adult life in society. This focus on childhood stresses a continuity of being in Schreiner's characters, enabling her to offer an analysis of experience that combines nature and nurture. Elements of the humor and the farcical external treatment of Bonaparte Blenkins in *African Farm* show some debt to Dickens, too, as do details and characters in *Undine*. *Jane Eyre* might have had something to do with the portrait of the hypocritical Blenkins and with the punishment, anger, and eloquence of a young girl in *African Farm*.[14] The "erotic movement toward annihilation" carried by a pubescent girl and the focus on a child victim who can later become the "little mother" (Spilka, 174–77), which we now perceive as symptoms of Victorian repression and its consequent sentimentality, are other recurring elements in Schreiner's fictions. They attest to the power of the repressive evangelical environment that engendered her struggles in the first place. Jane P. Tompkins has argued that novels like Stowe's *Uncle Tom's Cabin* should be revalued for the way in which they represented "a monumental effort to reorganize culture from the woman's point of view"; sentimental fictions were political enterprises "halfway between sermon and social theory."[15] The features of these fictions—the power of the dead or dying to redeem an unregenerate world, the tears and gestures that point to salvation and reconciliation, and "religious conversion as the necessary precondition for sweeping social change" (p. 89)—belong to eschatological vision and typological narrative. Human history is seen as a "continual reenactment of the drama of redemption" (p. 91).

Schreiner's depictions of "fallen women" in Lyndall and Bertie (in *From Man to Man*) align her fictional enterprises with those of Thomas Hardy, especially *Tess of the D'Urbervilles* (1891). Like Hardy, she wanted to represent the "sexual relationship as it is" rather than as promulgated by conventional Victorian morality (Ardis, 34). Writing candidly about women's desires and conflicts, Schreiner, like Hardy and Ibsen, sought to explode a false morality by depicting the suffering and lack of choice of empathetically rendered, virtuous heroines. She noted that Hardy's *A Pair of Blue Eyes* (1873) contained an episode that closely resembled a situation in *From Man to Man:* that of a woman who is rejected by the man she loves and wishes to marry when she confesses to him an earlier relationship. (SCCS, *Letters,* 14). Many of Schreiner's discussions with Havelock Ellis in the early eighties were about her reading and her responses to radical social protest in new fiction and drama by Hardy and especially by Ibsen, both his *A Doll's House* (first translated by Frances Lord as "Nora") and his *Ghosts*. What Ibsen offered her was a strengthening belief that the difficulties of love relationships could be openly depicted, that "some sides of a woman's nature that are not often spoken of" could be artistically handled, and that "men suffer as much as women from the falseness of the relations" (Rive, *Letters,* 36,37). *Ghosts* impressed her with its outspokenness on taboo subjects such as incestuous love and its attention to "the question of equal moral laws for both sexes" (Rive, *Letters,* 49). Schreiner's focus on the "double standard" and her recognition that the lives of both sexes were distorted by a false morality and polarized sex roles would remain constant features of her feminism and social vision.

Another feature of her personality and work, one with damaging consequences for her life and her writing, was a close identification with victims and a lifelong concern with suffering. This emerges in her comment on Hardy's style, that he is too impersonal, "only fingering his characters with his hands, not pressing them up against him till he felt their hearts beat" (Rive, *Letters,* 35). This criticism echoes Charlotte Brontë's response to Jane Austen's treatment of her characters (Armstrong, 45). A similar sentimentality runs through her response to Eliot's translation of Strauss's life of Jesus (translated 1846), which "made me love Jesus so much. I never cried over the crucifixion till I read Strauss's cold dispassionate criticism of that poor loving human soul that had been so tender to others, left there to face death alone" (Rive, *Letters,* 3). As Ellis pointed out to her, morbid charnel-house feelings of guilt and fear remained part of her sensibility, as did a need for self-renunciation, an inheritance from her preaching ancestors.[16] She speaks in maternal and feminine terms of her characters and stories, as if they were her children: *The Story of an African Farm* (in her dedication of the second edition to her friend Mary Brown) is "this little firstling of my pen" (see Monsman, 80). Dorothy Driver has discussed this maternal, biological strain in Schreiner's writing as a feminist forerunner of the radical critique offered by the French school of "écriture féminine," which feminizes metaphors of female creativity, making it "a cultural act."[17]

The writer with whom Schreiner identified when first in England, particularly when she was suffering from asthma and a host of related physical and psychological complaints, was Heinrich Heine, confined to his bed by a paralytic illness for the last eight years of his life: "I personify myself with him" (Rive, *Letters,* 38). Ellis translated Heine's poetry and prose and shared Schreiner's enthusiasm (Rive, *Letters,* 38). In these affiliations Schreiner reveals a Romantic cult of sensibility that surfaces in her writing, particularly in her treatment of death scenes in *Undine* and *African Farm.* The projected ending of *From Man to Man* would also have combined the death scene of a "fallen woman" with a vision of future sexual harmony. The sacrificial death of the "fallen woman" is always a visionary moment in which a secular dream of Spencerian progress toward greater relational harmony is prophesied. In Schreiner's work, such scenes and figures represent a drive toward self-immolation that coexists with a drive toward self-fulfillment, a conflict "central to middle class Victorian women's artistic struggles."[18] Historical figures like George Eliot and George Sand, whom Schreiner and many of her contemporaries admired for their combination of "masculine" intellect and "feminine" sensibility, of head and heart, are refracted through Schreiner's works in an array of fragmented positions that express a sense of threatened identity, female powerlessness, and distorting social arrangements. The colonial and personal circumstances of Schreiner's life framed and intensified such powerlessness and marginality but were also the basis of her creative empathy and the visionary narratives that prophesied release for women. Another key modulation of available Victorian discourses lies in Schreiner's skeptical response to the excesses of imperial romances and sensationalist fictions. Her novels can be read as the obverse of Rider Haggard's male romance quests, figured as a penetration of an exotic, sexualized landscape in search of treasure by a group of male adventurers. Schreiner's topics are difficult inner quests by women or feminized men in search of spiritual truth and wholeness of being within a culture that denies tenderness and imagination to men, and intellect and autonomy to women. Her response to exoticism is explicitly articulated in her preface to the second edition of *African Farm*, where wild creatures and narrow escapes (the stuff of her own earlier tales to children) are rejected for the somber realism of local colors and conditions: The writer must "paint what lies before him" (*SAF*, preface, 24). Although this might seem to refer to external landscapes and local colors, what lies before this particular colonial artist are the lives and fates of talented colonial youth, especially those "colonized" female questions about religious authority, marriage, male dominance, double standards, and specific colonial cultural conditions pertaining to education, labor, and race. Rider Haggard's *King Solomon's Mines* (1885) can be read as "a contorted attempt to resolve . . . the economic and psychosexual anxieties swirling around the riddles of female labour, sexuality, and male generative power in the Victorian metropolis; and, second, anxieties about female labour and sexuality in the colonies" writes Anne McClintock.[19] Schreiner's fictions represent the obverse of Haggard's quest: narratives spun from the lives of colonial female subjects living out the contradictions of exploited labor and sexuality, forms of exploitation constantly interconnected in her writings as they were in Schreiner's own life.

Schreiner's response to her own experience and reading is to weave her narratives around herself as projected romantic heroine.[20] This involves a focus on women's experience and on female or feminized storytellers and listeners, people who are marginal to the transactions of land and power in the colony. Female narrative transmission is substituted for the typically male form as found, for instance, in Conrad's *Heart of Darkness* (1902), which critiques the damage wrought by imperialism in Africa. In *Heart of Darkness* (written a few years after Schreiner's *Trooper Peter Halket of Mashonaland*, 1897), Kurtz's story of moral disintegration under the pressure of "savagery" is confided first to Marlow and later to the circle of listening sailors aboard the yawl *Nellie*. Kurtz's story is withheld from "The Intended," his fiancée, who is treated with sardonic scorn by Marlow because she cannot be entrusted with the burden of male suffering in Africa or indeed in any colonial outpost where the "true stuff" of the British moral tradition is tested and sometimes found wanting. Women are simultaneously seen as idealistic creatures who are unworthy of the corrosive truth, who in fact have to be protected from that truth, and who are contemptible because they live in a separate, illusionary space where male chivalry has traditionally kept them. Conrad writes within a highly evolved form of male romantic quest and for a conservative, male readership of *Blackwood's Edinburgh Magazine*, which subjected women to such self-contradictory standards. Male homosocial bonding determined forms of narrative transmission and forms of exclusion from stories. Narrative transmission echoed the patrilineal transmission of wealth and land in the British Empire; Em's inheriting of her stepmother's farm in South Africa (in *African Farm*) is anomalous in this context—one of Schreiner's many inversions of the norm. Contrasting with Conrad's narrative paradigms, Schreiner's fictions often have scenes of empowering narrative transmission between women, a pattern particularly marked in *Undine* and "Diamond Fields," where an older independent woman tells stories to a younger crippled girl. Storytelling between women is always a moment of shared understanding, peace, and reciprocity in Schreiner's works, an image of the act of creative empathy in which she is engaged as author. Female narrative transactions—which are varied and have multiple functions—are thus substituted for the male transactions of imperialistic romance, or, in Nina Auerbach's formulation, they "engorge the patriarchy" through speech and writing itself (to use one of Schreiner's own "eating" metaphors), transfusing "an oppressive world into its own mythmaking substance" (Auerbach, 159).

Schreiner's narratives thus disrupt the patterns of male romantic quest or adventure stories that have exploration, domination, or destruction as their goal and in which landscape is penetrated and colonized. In Schreiner's stories a young girl often ventures outside the traditional family house into the landscape and finds a place of her own that is usually bounded, peaceful, natural, and "free" (Schoeman, 440–41). Here she achieves peace with herself and begins to imagine an interested listener. The stories or ideas can be more or less evolved, more or less intellectual or imaginative. Typically, this space is within an African landscape, a kloof—a path or clearing associated with the solitude and freedom of childhood outside the home—but it can also be a space adjacent to but separate from family duties, like Rebekah's small study next to her children's bedroom in *From Man to Man*. Such places bring to mind the small areas in Victorian society within which an independent female ego could develop. Whether Eastern Province bush-world, the karoo, diamond fields, London slums, public colonial ballrooms, farmhouses, or bedrooms—all these settings play different roles in Schreiner's writings, representing as they do the clash between individual aspiration and the world of social norms, restricted or promising freedoms, social failures and outcast positions, confinement or liberation. Growing up in a landscape possessing a certain wild freedom, Schreiner was herself never fully socialized or adapted to pressing urban communities and mass existence.[21] This was one of the reasons she so often fled from human beings and their demands. The restrictions of society—and even of clothing—represented a kind of death that she and her characters constantly struggle to escape.

Although Schreiner writes in support of her own somber "realism" in her preface to *African Farm*, the genre she was rejecting or modulating was the Victorian three-decker in which linear structures and plot development reflected "genealogical fables of inheritance, marriage and death" (Showalter, 18). Like other late Victorians, she "questioned beliefs in endings and closures, as well as in marriage and inheritance" (Showalter, 18).[22] She also questioned naturalism in her crossovers between dreams and real life, allegory and realism in her scenes of African farm life. She was writing at a time when the publishing and novel-writing scene was evolving toward more flexible single forms and the fluid symbolist forms of the fin de siècle; she helped to shape that movement with her emphasis on allegory and vision, particularly in the writing she did in the late eighties. Her narratives approach moments of peace or rupture but never settle into the stability of a marriage symbolizing individual maturation or social bonding. In *From Man to Man* the heroine's maturity would be marked by her ability to negotiate for independence within conventional marriage. Even Schreiner's death scenes are more like random dissolutions than actual deaths. Her heroines' longing for romantic love and protective care coexist with a recognition of marriage as essentially a property transaction inseparable from social inequality and gender imbalance. Her novels "reject both the familiar patterning of the marriage plot and the cultural endorsement of marriage as the means by which 'patterns of passion and patterns of property' are always 'brought into harmonious alignment' " (Tanner, cited by Ardis, 60–61).

Schreiner's critical preface to *African Farm* tells us that her narratives do not work according to "the stage method" but according to the random arrivals and departures of friends and strangers "where there is a strange coming and going of feet" (*SAF,* preface, 23). We see fragmented scenes of difficult and broken lives, crossed by dreams and fantasies, interrupted by extended polemical discourses, long female complaints in letters, and internal narrative exchanges, thus calling any master narrative into question and the patterns of patrilineal inheritance they symbolize. Social codes for sexual behavior are challenged and deconstructed, scenes of courtship and romance are parodied by role reversals and cross-dressings, forced or illegitimate partnerships, kept women or masterful women, passive men, and ruptured sexual and social bonds. The myth of the absence of female passion is discarded: "I like to try" says Lyndall. Bertie tells of the pleasure of being loved by men; Rebekah crawls into the bed of her faithless husband for physical comfort. As Showalter argues, the last decade of the nineteenth century saw "new sexual and fictional combinations" (Showalter, 16). Schreiner's outspokenness about female desire and sexual behavior was one of the catalysts in this process. At the same time, her fictions and polemics reveal a contrary and more traditional desire to assimilate sexual love to maternal affection or a childlike lack of passion.[23] There is, too, the wider question of whether narratives of sexual illegitimacy conceal or blur the problem of female autonomy.

Thus, although at one level Schreiner challenges "romance" and its distortions of the colonial realities that lay before her, at another level she challenges mimeticism and reinstalls fantasy, surrendering herself to strange imaginings that she must have realized would instinctively embody the contradictions of the age: "I have just painted such a singular scene," she writes, after completing the episode in which Veronica Gray goes into a man's room and strokes his clothes and brushes.[24] Dreams and allegories, in their secular reworkings of Bunyanesque moral allegory, could tell a new kind of truth about those marginal beings in the colonies the Puritans went forth to conquer and convert. This truth would be deeply tied to "an intense ambivalence towards traditional male-female relationships" (Armstrong, 193), even as Schreiner constructed the fictions that represented a partial triumph over that ambivalence.

Undine: Olive Schreiner's "Lehrjahre"

Of Schreiner's four novels, only *The Story of an African Farm* (1883) and *Trooper Peter Halket of Mashonaland* (1897) were published in her lifetime. Her first completed novel, *Undine* (first published in 1928), and her incomplete novel, *From Man to Man* (1926), were both published posthumously and thus have filled out the portrait of her writing life only in retrospect. They had no consequences for those who lived in Schreiner's day, although they may well have had some effect on the shaping of a subsequent feminist consciousness and historical understanding of her period and her position in it. Both texts are interesting additions to her oeuvre and our understanding of the complex relationship between her life and her writing.

Undine allows us to see Schreiner's first encounter with the conventions of the novel as she understood them, and her first attempt to transform the data of autobiography into representative narratives. Set in South Africa between 1872 and 1881, the novel serves as a touchstone for Schreiner's other two novels about young colonial women and shows the nature of her artistic struggles with her material. Although she regarded it as unworthy of publication and said that only "the biographical element" made her look kindly upon it at all (Draznin, 219–20), the novel is an intriguing revelation of hesitancy and control in her life and art, of complex self-divisions that were common to many women of her time.

Related to her conception of herself as an English-South African working with a metropolitan mode in a colonial outpost, the first form of hesitation concerned the setting of the novel. In *Undine* she seems to hanker after the English landscapes of Hardy, Eliot, and the Brontës and

appears to believe that only a novel set mainly in England would be valued by an educated reading public. The landscapes they knew so intimately were known to her only through reading (the metropolitan literary inheritance is figured in the trove of books Waldo finds in the loft in
African Farm). Having no real experience of England, she creates a
loosely defined village called Greenwood and transposes to that setting
some of the personal conflicts she knew from her association with
authoritarian, hypocritical Wesleyans, loved but socially inaccessible
men, and envious, gossiping women in small colonial towns. Conventional middle-class colonial society did in any case imitate English life
and manners, as her scenes set on board ship to Africa show. Only at the
beginning and in the last section of the novel are events set in Africa;
the last section has both a journey by oxcart and incidents at the Diamond Fields along the Vaal River in the Transvaal, then called New
Rush, which she knew well from having lived there with her elder brother
and sister from December 1872 to October 1873. There is a recognizable gain in immediacy and detail once the setting moves to Port Elizabeth and New Rush, center of the diamond discoveries that changed the
face of the Cape Colony and South Africa. *Undine* was thus a testing of
locales and settings and establishes the trope of a circular journey
between Africa and England in which remembered landscapes coexist
with everyday experience. Later, with more knowledge and experience
of England, Schreiner would describe Bertie in London when she was
extensively revising *From Man to Man*, but by then England had become
a real place from which African landscapes would be recalled with great
yearning and loss.

In *Undine*, too, Schreiner was still working more extensively with the
genre of fairy tales and with what she knew of sensationalist fiction.
Fairy tales are often referred to in the novel and were forbidden reading
for the young Undine. Baron de la Motte Fouqué's *Undine* has many
parallels with Schreiner's novel: a water nymph unfortunate on land and
sea, wicked relatives, and a struggle to obtain a human soul. Monsman
points out that in *Undine* Schreiner merged the fairy tale structure "with
the novel of doctrine and manners" (p. 38) but that the treatment of
material is derivative. She had read Ouida's highly romanticized novel
Tricotrin (Schoeman, 412); her own early children's stories were thrilling
tales of adventures and dangerously close escapes, carrying her own
sense of danger and defenselessness into fantasy.

She was caught up, like so many others, in the excitement of the diamond discoveries, and one of her earliest stories, written in November

1872, was "The Story of a Diamond" (SCCS, *Life*, 10). In *Undine*, however, literary melodrama prevails: Undine's Aunt Margaret goes mad and attacks Undine; her brother dies by drowning; both Alice Brown and her child die by drowning; Undine's child dies; and Undine herself contemplates suicide. Schreiner creates heartless marriages for mercenary reasons, deathbed nursings and declarations, and numerous entanglements between relatives, family, step family, and lovers. Havelock Ellis, to whom she gave the manuscript of *Undine*, asked her in polite bewilderment to explain the relationship between Frank and Aunt Margaret. The exhilarating atmosphere of the diamond fields and the heady sense of adventure and opportunity of that era seem to have triggered the desire to write more sensationalist fiction. Schreiner responded defiantly to Ellis about "New Rush," her later fragmented attempt in London to recast the diamond fields experience as a "sensational story." Ellis admired the scene of Aunt Margaret's madness in *Undine,* although to many it will read like the crudest melodrama. Such "mad scenes," however, convey the tension between family and sexual love that Schreiner knew in adolescence.

The male-female relationships in *Undine* are also extremely mechanistic, didactic, and self-sacrificing, although in their mechanisms and inversions they make explicit the actual basis of conventional courtship and of gender norms at the time. Undine's relationship with her cousin Jonathan, a married man who pours out his guilty love for her, is based on Schreiner's relationship with Zadoc Robinson, a Wesleyan minister who first formally employed her as governess and who lived in the small town of Dordrecht (1871–1872), where her disastrous relationship with Julius Gau developed. Cousin Jonathan, like Zadoc Robinson, is an older married guardian, spiritual mentor, and at first a trusted confidant. Much like the formative experience of Schreiner's adolescence and early womanhood, Undine's relationship with Jonathan conveys some of the claustrophobic sexuality and social unease of the situation of a young governess. The reason the central relationships are not clearer seems to be related to Schreiner's own youthful, confused reactions to family bonds, the moral superintendence of her elder brother and sister as surrogate parents, and her own sexual yearnings, rebellious intellect, and spiritual and social nonconformity.

The main relationship—that between Undine and Albert Blair—is closely modeled on Schreiner's disastrous experience with Julius Gau and the local gossip it generated. The younger effeminate brother and lover may have been modeled on Gau's own brother.[25] This would fit

Schreiner's own insistence on the autobiographical elements in the novel, but what is interesting is the cruder form of the sexual bargain the heroine strikes with the male figures in order to avoid any real engagement or commitment. Lyndall is willing to become engaged to a man she does not love but can control; she also consents first to give herself sexually to a "superior," powerful man and then to send him away when she most needs help and company. So also does Undine fall in love with Albert Blair, the cold-hearted "piece of perfection"; when Albert subsequently rejects her, she in turn rejects his younger, effeminate brother and marries his elderly, rich, unattractive father. She does this ostensibly to benefit Albert, who will be seen again only when he is dead and she can safely kiss his cold face. These plot contortions, although expressive within the fairy tale structure, also seem to express extremes of emotional need, fear, and self-evasion. They articulate the ways in which courtship and marriage were genuinely sterile and imprisoning for women and involved a destruction of female individuality and a stifling of creativity and independent activity for women. Blair's constant admonishments to Undine to curb her eccentricities and cultivate a genteel veneer may well have been based on Gau's attitude toward Schreiner herself and were not uncommon. The marriage bargain Undine strikes with George Blair, the rich father, an unattractive, authoritarian man, is melodramatic, but it reveals the desire for property and possession as a common basis of marriage; Schreiner, however, inverts the relationship by putting this mercenary decision in the hands of her heroine. The customary sexual commodification of women is thus pointedly converted into the sexual commodification of men.

In *Undine* other aspects of Schreiner's own experience are displaced onto different female figures with whom Undine has some relationship. Her own real or pseudopregnancy is displaced onto Albert Blair's other lover, Alice Brown, a beautiful lower-class woman who drowns herself after a visit by Undine, during which visit her illegitimate child by Albert Blair dies. Soon afterward Undine's own (legitimate) child dies. This doubling or transposition may reveal Schreiner's own situation in Dordrecht. Yet such stories of illegitimacy and the deaths of young abandoned mothers and babies seem to validate Victorian morality. Illegitimacy is purified by death or sacrifice ; the metaphor of childbirth confirms mothers as fallen women.[26] It has been argued, however, that childbirth as metaphor opens up a "potential space . . . to think about the nature of human beings within a biological system which must use sexuality as a means of continuation but also assigns it a social familial value" (MacPike, 56). The contrast between the self-righteous colonial, Mrs. Snappercaps, and her fat children, whom she slaps or ignores, and the deaths of Alice Brown and Undine's children, opens up a space for the ethical investigation of the role of childbirth within and outside marriage. Alice Brown's love child is further contrasted with Undine's child of an apparently mercenary bargain with an older man, but one concealing exalted self-sacrifice for a worthless lover. These complicated plotlines involving the inheritance of wealth (Undine renounces her inherited wealth in favor of the two Blair sons) underline the close connection between conventional social morality and material wealth: The double standard of sexual behavior was based on male fears of losing wealth to illegitimate children. By relocating value to children outside the legality of marriage and patrilineal inheritance and endowing their deaths with loss and pathos, scenes of apparent melodrama called attention to a new value system for women and children, one based on love and individual value rather than property inheritance. *Undine*'s primary motif—"King Gold"—is a thematic and structural opposition between Mammon and spiritual value (242–43).

The story of covert love for a married man may have been based on Schreiner's relationship with George Weakley, her second employer, who seems to have exploited her as a labor resource but who "exerted a strange fascination over her" (Ellis, "Notes"). Her experience is displaced onto the "shabby woman" with beautiful gray eyes whom Undine meets on the boat traveling back to South Africa from England and who tells Undine her story. These other female protagonists and their stories are thus uttered in internal narratives, secrets in lockets, and scandalous rumors of illegitimacy. These are superseded by the final story of Undine at the Diamond Fields as an independent working woman who can comfort the crippled girl Diogenes by telling her wonderful stories. Narrative transactions between women, especially women who carry the burden of destructive authorial experiences, seem to be liberating and empowering, even though the novel has a sensationalistic ending. In *Undine* the conventions of melodrama and fantasy carry the inner secret stories of dependent women who love unattainable men, experience sexuality in circumstances of guilt or illegitimacy, and are exploited as a cheap labor resource by jealous and bullying women. The dependence that makes female employers hateful but endows male employers with an ambivalent attraction is broken only when Undine becomes an independent wage earner, an ironing lady at the Fields, in the last section of the novel. This movement dramatizes one of Schreiner's own heartfelt cries when she was a governess: "How glorious to be in the power of no woman" ("Lily Kloof" journal entry, Clayton, 106). Schreiner frequently expatiated on the dangers of economic dependence for any love relationship and struggled to maintain her own economic independence. The unlikelihood of Undine's washerwoman existence at the Fields emphasizes how few outlets there were for women economically and how the only way for a white middle-class woman to achieve economic independence was to become working class. Undine speaks of a defection from her own class in the novel and is always represented as a perfect lady, in contrast to her nouveau riche colonial employer, Mrs. Snappercaps. Here Schreiner's own ambivalent class position as the impoverished daughter of a cultured missionary family is relevant. Furthermore, Nancy Armstrong points out that "the governess . . . combines certain features of the aristocracy with those of the working woman" and "by fulfilling the duties of the domestic woman for money . . . she blurred a distinction on which the very notion of gender appeared to depend." (Armstrong, 79) Schreiner's ambiguous position as family friend/governess/dependant/servant in the households in which she lived between 1871 and 1881 intensified self-doubts and vulnerability, resulting in a sometimes excessive hauteur born of humiliation and often directed at English Afrikaners and indigenous races. Spiritual superiority or the superiority of beauty were available even to someone who was poorer and hungrier than the most miserable native at the fields, as Undine finds herself to be.

This ambiguous class position coincided with confusion about family and romantic love and an uncertainty about gender roles when a passionate young girl was suddenly expected to earn her living like a man without having any of the freedom or education of a man. At the same time Schreiner's year at Dordrecht was a year of extraordinary personal growth, during which she framed the key questions that would occupy her throughout her life:

Why should a woman not break through conventional restraints that enervate her mind and dwarf her body, and enjoy a wild, free, true life, as a man may?—wander the green world over by the help of hands and feet, and lead a free rough life in bondage to no man?—forget the old morbid loves and longings?—live and enjoy and learn as much as may before the silence comes? (p. 243)

The answer to this question is articulated by Undine herself: She was

free to feel that a woman is a poor thing carrying in herself the bands
that bind her ... and how long would she be able to maintain herself
without getting under someone's thumb? ... As it was, being only a
woman and with the scent not yet out of her hair nor the softness rubbed
from her hands, she stood there in the street, feeling very weak, bodily,
after her illness, and mentally, after her long life of servitude and dependence—very weak and very heartsick. (pp. 245–46)

Undine is thus ideologically torn between extremes of feminine behavior, including the most abject angel in the house who sees all misfor-
tunes as her own fault and constantly seeks expiation for uncommitted
sins through nursing and financial self-sacrifice, and feminist assertions
that examine the causes of gendered divisions of labor and the relegation
of women to the private sphere of domestic labor.

Moreover, in this early novel there is very little awareness of racial
victimization; the "Kaffir" and "Hottentot" as well as the Jewish diamond merchants are objects of contempt and scorn, and the "half-civilized," fashionable black gentleman is seen stereotypically as inevitably
comic or considerably more evil than a true "savage."[27] Black laundry-
women are thieves; ladies forced into ironing tasks are the real victims of
society. In *Undine* the fact that blacks were the true diggers and were
being subordinated by white diggers and agents is noted, but many of
the narrative reflections simply echo the conventional "wisdom" and terminology of the times. Schreiner's maturation would bring more awareness of racial discrimination and exploitation, but her three novels written as a youth have a martyred young white girl at the center. Young
white children are portrayed as the true victims, which is made clear in
the relationship between Undine and Diogenes, her young friend whose
back was broken by her mother's beating the night before she died in
childbirth. Schreiner's works are thus, at one level, disguised accusations
of her family for authoritarian and punitive behavior. Parents or their
surrogates are absent, tyrannical, or cruel, and the sadistic beating of
Diogenes in *Undine* is an even more extreme version of Waldo's flogging
in *African Farm*. "A child is being beaten" is Freud's heading for a discussion of Oedipal fantasies and fantasized scenes of punishment.[28] Parental
love and punishment had been closely associated for Schreiner, and even
her own ambivalent love for women seems to be connected with this
fact. They were both objects of erotic interest and admiration and spite-
ful tyrants and rivals. The contempt shown for effeminate men such as
Harry Blair in *Undine* seems to be a displaced contempt for her feminized self, a woman who often experienced social censure for being

"masculine" in her intellectual aspirations "to know" and in relation to more conventional women living in a charmed circle of class, wealth, and male protection, like the fair woman who is the "gem" surrounded by attention and wealth in the rich section of New Rush (293).

Undine is thus an apprentice novel. Schreiner worked steadily at it in a rather detached way but was always unsure whether it would be worth publishing because of its strong autobiographical elements and its immaturity. Ellis noted that it was nicely done but almost entirely without her characteristic voice and quite wooden in relation to the achievement and assurance of *African Farm* (Draznin, 83). She herself knew when starting her "other work" that it would be much better than "poor little *Undine*." (Ratel Hoek journal, Clayton, 104). According to Schreiner, the theme of the book was "the story of a woman who begins life [with] a wild passionate nature full of longings for love and knowledge and sympathy; and slowly she learns to renounce, and renounce and renounce" (Rive, *Letters*, 76). She sent the ending of the novel to Karl Pearson almost as a disguised confession of love and of her own experience, which was a fairly typical proceeding for her, but added: "I don't know what I drag them about with me for. I often try to burn them, and it gives me such pain. It seems as if I were burning the people in them. And yet I am afraid they will publish them after I am dead" (Rive, *Letters*, 76).

Nevertheless, *Undine* is notable as a sensitive young girl's recasting of a historical crux in South African history: the finding of mineral wealth that transformed the country from a rural backward economy into an industrialized nation and the making of a strange new landscape and heterogeneous community. She vividly describes New Rush, where the stirrings of labor power and organization could be seen, where the old frontier hostilities between Boer and black were being redrawn, and where English colonial pretensions to culture and refinement were being tested and exposed in new circumstances. The bustle and activity at New Rush, the strange beauty of the mine itself in moonlight, like a medieval vision full of glamour and romance, and the sense of a new conglomerate, multiracial community being formed around a search for wealth and hope are all vivid elements of *Undine:*

> She sat down to rest on the side of one of the mountains of gravel between which the road passed, and, when the camp below was aglow with evening lights, and the noise and stir in its tents and streets became louder and stronger, she rose up and walked into the Kop in the bright

moonlight. It was like entering the city of the dead in the land of the living, so quiet it was, so well did the high-piled gravel heaps keep out all sound of the seething noisy world around. Not a sound, not a movement. She walked to the edge of the reef and looked down into the crater. The thousand wires that crossed it, glistening in the moonlight, formed a weird, sheeny, mistlike veil over the black depths beneath. Very dark, very deep it lay all round the edge, but, high towering into the bright moonlight, rose the unworked centre. She crouched down at the foot of the staging and sat looking at it. In the magic of the moonlight it was a giant castle, a castle of the olden knightly days; you might swear, as you gazed on it, that you saw the shadows of its castellated battlements, and the endless turrets that overcrowned it: a giant castle, lulled to sleep and bound in silence for a thousand years by the word of some enchanter. You might gaze until you almost saw the ivy clinging to its yellow crumbling walls, till you almost saw the figures of brave knights and lovely ladies, whom the death-like sleep had overtaken as they wandered on the castle terraces, till the motionless horse and the small arched window and the mighty dragon resting in the gateway were all visible. (*Undine,* 297–98)

Here, in the ability to render and imaginatively transform scenes hitherto unrecorded amid emergent South African realities, lies Schreiner's greatest contribution to South African literature. Similarly, in placing one of her characters in a miner's tent, she offers us a catalogue of objects that convey an intimate portrait of an era and a place—and of male migrancy:

On the sea-chest that stood in the middle of the tent was such a multifarious and miscellaneous collection of articles as surely sea-chest never bore before. There were tins and bottles of every description, the latter crowned with the remains of half burnt candles; there were old newspapers and shoe blacking, books and a pepper caster, pens and cigar ends, a paint box and a broken looking glass, a microscope and combs, hair brushes, tooth brushes, boot brushes, nail brushes and a papier mache desk on which was a sliver-clasped album across which lay the broken head of a pick; these with an infinitude of other smaller and larger articles covered it. (*Undine,* 331)

Such documentary passages depict the life of the times in objects as well as the historical pathos of the (white) diggers. Objects are composed into scene paintings by achieving a degree of distance: "Undine . . . sauntered off to a little distance among the bushes, where she could

have a good view of the waggon as it showed in the light of the blazing
fire" (*Undine*, 258). Conversations and characters are created; clusters of
narrative symbols are built up around snow and water and "King Gold."
The medieval motif of knights and ladies in impossible romance is maintained through alternating realistic description and allegory. The painting described in some detail early in the novel has its pattern and
prophecy fulfilled in the final developments of the main plot. The scenes
at New Rush would be recast later in her unfinished "Diamond
Fields"—with a strong independent woman, Monica St. John, as the
main character—while Schreiner was in England in 1882. In *Undine*
Schreiner was working with fantasy and autobiography, allegory and
realism, learning when to have a character become narrator (the maid
Nancy, for instance) and how to structure chapters and include indigenous songs or local speech. South African culture was being accepted as
worthy of serious fictional representation for the first time.

The style is still rather stilted and ornate, compared with *African
Farm*. Character links and doublings, contrasts and shadowy parallels,
are worked up to offer variations on the theme of female rebellion, disillusionment, and renunciation. The main interest lies in the insertion of a
young female subject into the predominantly male historical narrative of
South African history at the moment at which the old Africa was giving
way to the new:

> Africa, as it appeared in that desolate and sandsmitten seaport, was not
> the Africa of her memory. The old Africa with its great grass and karoo
> flats and rough rock-crowned mountains, unridden and un-man-defiled
> old Africa, was little like the sand-smothered town in which she stood,
> which might have been in any country in Europe but for the ragged nig-
> gers slouching about the streets and the dark, dirty, half-clothed fishboys
> who dragged their wares along with tails draggling in the sand. (*Undine*,
> 244)

Africa was taking on the lineaments of an industrialized landscape, one
in which divisions between English colonials and Afrikaners, between
whites and blacks would harden as the struggle for wealth and the control of wealth intensified. The narrative voice and viewpoint of *Undine*
reveals the stereotypic attitudes of English colonials at the time while
simultaneously questioning the subservience of women to male norms in
a manner that had implications for other exploited races and classes. In
particular, the commodification of women as marriage property is challenged and inverted, portraying the powerlessness of women to effect

any relationships on their own terms. Female education is shown up for the paltry "training" it was.

Many of these tropes and scenes would recur in *African Farm* with more force and vitality: The oxwagon journey in *Undine* is, however, a wonderful insight into the actual discomforts of contemporary African domestic travel "before the first tramway is set" ("DF," 15). The trope of the beaten child, the rebellious, nonconformist little girl with a strong will, the circular journey between England and Africa, the socially disgraced woman and her dead child, the gossiping Christian women, the intertextual references to Herbert Spencer and John Stuart Mill, an African landscape transformed by moonlight or bringing mystical peace and harmony, the desire for immortality, the drive toward dissolution and death, are all prefigured in *Undine*. In particular, the mystical moment in a healing African landscape is given its first symbolic form. Feminist questions are still tentative, however, and are overwhelmed in the subduing of the story to the mythology of female martyrdom and disappointed romantic love. In *African Farm* the voice of the radical questioning woman would be given more space. In *Undine* what we see is that in the industrial crucible of colonial South Africa, there was almost no space for independent women outside marriage, and Undine's death symbolizes the hopelessness of female autonomy under such circumstances of outward disapproval and a conditioned subservience. Female subjectivity is revealed as deeply divided in its need for love and independence: The movement of the novel between extremes of rebellion and self-immolation dramatizes the agonizing copresence of these opposed needs.

In *The Story of an African Farm* the contradictory discourses of feminism and femininity are given a more impersonal and artistic form, but in *Undine*, because of its autobiographical nature, we find much poignant insight into the actual problems and extreme vulnerability of a young colonial author. We observe her with interest and compassion during her formative years at Dordrecht and the Diamond Fields. Here she encounters both the dangers of illegitimate sexuality and the promise, within the burgeoning economic activity of South Africa, of creative activity that could deliver her from virtual bondage to the romance of a writer's life.

Chapter Three

Courtship and Marriage in the Colonies:
The Story of an African Farm

At the genesis of industrialization in South Africa—as the old Africa was making way for the new—Olive Schreiner's works addressed the issue of colonialism. She did so by exposing the plight of young colonial women under patriarchal, religious, and social authority. The effect of her efforts was the creation of a modern consciousness of power, injustice, and complicity with injustice. In *Undine* the derivative literary structures, the vague English setting, and a sentimental emphasis on female martyrdom impede the full expression of her awareness of oppression in South Africa. Ellis remarked to Schreiner on the "magnitude of the step" between *Undine* and *African Farm*, the former quite wooden and without her characteristic individual voice, the latter altogether full of "intellectual power" and "power of artistic expression" (Draznin, 250). In *African Farm* an emergent feminist consciousness is given broader expression, despite the occasional complicity of the novel with patriarchal norms. *The Story of an African Farm* may be considered the linchpin of Schreiner's œuvre and the mainspring of several literary and sociopolitical trends in South Africa and Europe. In the novel, an isolated colonial woman writer deliberately set about revising current patriarchal perspectives and discourses and inscribed a courageously honest personal voice and perspective to which generations of readers have responded in an intimate and impassioned way.[1] Literary, personal, and political elements have often been strongly enmeshed with one another in these responses.

The process of composition involved the drafts of several stories, one of which became *The Story of an African Farm* and another an early version of *From Man to Man* (called "Saints and Sinners" in its earlier stages). The novel's evolution is somewhat obscure and was not tied to one particular farm and date, despite Cronwright-Schreiner's creation of a myth of origin for the story. This is partly because of Schreiner's simultaneous work on three novels before she left South Africa in 1881, partly because of her confusing terminology ("writing" could often mean composing scenes orally while walking up and down, visualizing and verbalizing them), and partly because we have only journals and fragments of journals to restructure her intense and private creative processes. The origins of the two novels are hidden in the organic process by which several stories were emerging from the core experiences of the previous few years. Her writing was essentially a secretive process, concealed from prying eyes because she was already considered odd by colonial norms, and she felt so intimately connected with her characters and stories that to reveal them to others was a kind of betrayal. Nevertheless, she also desired to burst through the boundaries of colonial restriction and have some impact on a wider European world. This impulse toward self-assertion fought with her early, strict training in selflessness—the traditional "virtue" of women.

Many of the rituals practiced by Schreiner's young characters concern death and the appeasement of death and mortality, such as Waldo's youthful sacrifices to a disappearing God. Art was also one such ritual. In a family and at a time when infant mortality was high—her younger sister Ellie having been the most closely felt loss in her childhood—death was a constant threat, especially when her parents preached the inexorable judgment and eternal torments that death would bring to little sinners. In Schreiner's writings, "death is the foe of writing and writing the foe of death."[2] Narrative fertility staves off the process of time itself, and storytelling resists and transforms the relentlessness of history.

Although the relationship between early manuscripts and titles and later publications is sometimes confusing, the titles themselves echo her central preoccupations. "Other Men's Sins," which may have been an early title for "Saints and Sinners," addresses her continuing concern with a hypocritical community of Christians; the satirical thrust of the phrase conveys her desire to dismantle and overturn conventional moral judgments in the name of other values: honesty, charity, purity of heart, and the values of the Sermon on the Mount. [which no one in her family had found at all striking when, as a child, she ran in to tell them of her great discovery] (*SAF,* 129). Given the satirical emphasis on Blenkins as a crooked preacher, Tant Sannie as the mouthpiece of religious orthodoxy among the Boers, and the issues of sexual morality raised by Lyndall's illegitimate child, "Other Men's Sins" could almost equally refer to *The Story of an African Farm.* This is because both novels were a critique of conventional Christian morality and of the hypocritical gap between public morality and private behavior, especially in relation to sexuality.

This issue had cauterized Schreiner's youth and adolescence. Two stories—"Wrecked" and "A Small Bit of Mimosa"—that Schreiner had considered combining into one in "Saints and Sinners" focus on the life of a shipwrecked female in the Karoo landscape, where mimosas—the yellow thornbushes that characterize the landscape—serve as a motif and mnemonic. Another title, "Thorn Kloof" (mentioned in *African Farm* and the name of the childhood farm in *From Man to Man*), reveals that the imaginative rendering of a farm is central to her original conceptions of these two novels. Lyndall, Bertie, and Rebekah grow up on farms in the karoo; particular farm landscapes are part of their identities and memories, the bedrock of their continuing, struggling lives, and the landscape of a lost childhood. Farm landscapes, however, have different symbolic functions within the two texts. Whereas the bare red sand and koppies (low, ironstone hills) of *African Farm* suggest an elemental desolation as well as an underlying strength, the flowering mimosas of the Eastern province farm in *From Man to Man* evoke the difficult flowering of English colonial womanhood and reflect the yearning provoked by exile in England—particularly a dismal urban life in London. One early title for *African Farm*, "Lyndall", reveals that Schreiner's female characters—both "myself and not myself"—were a strong element in her original conceptions of storytelling, and she always speaks of the characters as if they were almost real companions or intimate female friends. Her narratives, although not tied to conventional plotting, are inseparable from the lives of the central characters, who have recognizably different personalities and desires, like siblings within a large family, characters who respond differently to fate and circumstance: "We are only the wood, the knife that carves on us is the circumstance" (*SAF,* 240). Characters, like siblings, could be fundamentally consistent and yet change and grow: Her older sister Ettie was "my soft hearted sister who used to stroke my hair" (Draznin, 219–20), an unforgiving Puritan as an older guardian, and later almost as much of a Freethinker as Olive. A large family of determined individuals, like the Schreiners, provided some of the material for the comparative insights into character and fate that structure *African Farm* and *From Man to Man,* which are triple and dual protagonist novels. A recognition of the role played by "character" is part of the process by which growth and constraints on fulfillment are fictionalized.

This multiple protagonist structure provided a more complex view of identity than the single protagonist pattern of *Undine. African Farm,* still under the sway of male societal norms, utilizes a male protagonist,

Waldo, as a major carrier of visionary understanding. By shifting the focus to two sisters in *From Man to Man,* a feminist critique of social norms and colonial fates for women could be further developed and embroidered.

By the time Schreiner was conceiving and working up the stories that eventually became the *African Farm* and incomplete *From Man to Man,* she had shifted from the Diamond Fields and small South African towns she knew and portrayed in *Undine* to the sequence of isolated karoo farms in the Cradock area (where she was a governess between 1875 and 1881): Klein Gannahoek, Ratelhoek, and Leliekloof. The slightly differing farm landscapes had several characteristics in common: a traditional, fairly uneducated Boer way of life that is both satirically and seriously handled, for different effects; English colonial farming families (like her friends the Cawoods, sometimes called "English Afrikaners," whose daughters may have been one source of Schreiner's emphasis on young female potential in the karoo); demoralized and exploited indigenous servants and laborers from the broken tribes of the Cape frontier wars; and the features of the farm itself: a bare farmhouse with its loft, sheep kraals, ostrich camps, ironstone koppies, and the surrounding landscape, often bare red sand, scrub, aloes, and mimosa bushes. Although this bare and unpromising environment was "home" in the sense that Schreiner knew and loved it well and spent happy active years here, these same surroundings frame and anchor her stories of talented young colonial people who are beaten by "the adverse material conditions of life"[3] and prevailing gender norms. The multitude of forms these adverse conditions could take on a South African farm are fully presented in Schreiner's writings, consciously and unconsciously; they present a microcosm of South African contemporary history and culture. On these farms, Schreiner tasted the misery of dependence but also the joy of being needed and valued as a teacher and cast her earlier experience of sexuality, "education," colonial social norms, and Christian hypocrisy into new forms. She tried to construct narratives that would express her sense of childhood outrage and liveliness, the trust young women place in romantic love and marriage and their consequent disillusionment, and an underlying quest to understand the place of the modern individual within a cosmic order bereft of a Christian God. Her impassioned outrage at the injustices she intimately knew would speak to the world at a time when organized resistance to imperialism, to capitalist and patriarchal systems, was in its infancy. It is in *The Story of an African Farm*—where the story and the farm, narratives and the life out

of which we spin narratives come into their own—that she was most
successful in shaping her familiar experience into art.

The Story of an African Farm: The Dark Mirror of the Mind

In *The Story of an African Farm*, which has had many passionate but varying critical responses, dream life and real life are complexly interwoven
so that both worlds, which are presented as equally "real" from the
opening scenes onward, are validated in relation to each other. The epigraph tells us that every human being is shaped by the first images that
are cast upon the "dark mirror of his mind;" the first chapter, "Shadows
from Child-life," illustrates this process in three strongly shaped
vignettes describing Waldo's early experience of religious terror, faith,
and abandonment. Identity is at once established as culturally formed
and yet a process of individual struggle against cultural formation. The
opening scene—in which the "full African moon poured down its light
from the blue sky into the wide, lonely plain"—presents us with paradoxical images of fullness and benevolence as well as desolation and a
hunger for fulfillment: "the milkbushes with their long, finger-like
leaves" offer one of the first of many images of a grasping out and
upward toward a desired communication between heaven and earth,
man and nature. The ironstone "kopje," a low rise in the plain where the
farm lies, is both mythical (a "giant's grave") and an actual heap of iron-
stones where Waldo will play out his agonizing religious conflict around
death, judgment, and faith. Here, too, a grown Lyndall will later tor-
ment her admirer, Gregory Rose. Images of different kinds of light are
woven through the opening scenes: the prickly pears that mirror the
moonlight, the "dreamy beauty" of the moonlight that "etherealized"
the farmhouse wall, the glint of ironstone and zinc suggesting harder
farm realities, transformed here until they "glinted with a quite peculiar
brightness, till it seemed that every rib in the metal was of burnished sil-
ver" (p. 29). The "weird but almost oppressive beauty" of this particular
colony has been established, and the constant juxtaposition of reflected
and transforming light suggests the interplay of individual and context,
reality and imagination, nature and art, with which the whole novel is
centrally concerned.

The mise-en-scène of the human dramas that unfold in the novel is
sketched: the approach to the farmhouse past sheep kraals and Kaffir
huts, where the betrayed, innocent Otto will ride; the homestead with

its thatched roof over which Waldo will clamber; the wooden ladder and the loft that will bear silent witness to many scenes of work, love, confession, betrayal, book searches, false accusations, revenge, and cross-dressings; the low stone walls that mark boundaries but do not fully conceal or protect. This firm continuing existence of inanimate objects, buildings, plants, spiders, beetles, and sand—the material world within which human aspirations are played out—is one of the novel's greatest strengths, suggesting a suffering and endurance both less and more than human. These objects and creatures link the human, natural, and manmade worlds into the complex whole that the characters discover beyond the shadows of experience. The farmhouse itself is a stage upon which the arbitrary play the author describes in her preface will be performed.

The key characteristics of the main actors are concisely described: Tant Sannie's complacent physicality and greed, and the contrast between elfin Lyndall and solid Em. Because Waldo is the central character at the beginning and end of the novel, one grasps the fact that he is a crusader on the cusp of modernity. His quest is for spiritual and moral certainties in the midst of Victorian doubt; for a scientific understanding of history and geography in South Africa, where so much has been destroyed and changed; for beauty and harmony where ignorant cruelty and intellectual deprivation are the rule; for technological progress in a climate of conservatism and suspicion. As a herdsboy and pastoralist who rejects orthodox Christianity as a result of searching philosophical questions, who seeks social justice and affection, who responds to organic relationships and sees them as the basis of a new aesthetic, Waldo is a vehicle for emergent nineteenth-century consciousness, like that of Schreiner's key mentor, John Stuart Mill (Waldo is punished for reading Mill's *Political Economy,* "your Polity-gollity-gominy, your devil's book," 105). At the end of the novel Waldo is also offered what Ellis called a Spencerian solution (Waldo's educated "stranger" gives him a copy of Spencer's *First Principles*): His pain at the loss of Lyndall and the finality of death are finally taken up and resolved as "his soul passed down the steps of contemplation into that vast land where there is always peace ... where the soul ... almost feels its hand on the old mystery of Universal Unity that surrounds it" (p. 271). The human cost of being the bearer of this new consciousness is drawn in the opening scenes, where, as a child, Waldo suffers the spiritual conflict of his times; his onerous task is resolved in the penultimate chapter, "Dreams."

Although the generational difference between old Otto and his son is representative of a Victorian shift in sensibility that would now be called a paradigm shift, the contest between old Otto and Bonaparte Blenkins is representative of another historical shift. A colonizing missionary presence is replaced by an overtly economic and exploitative imperialism carried by unscrupulous adventurers like Bonaparte Blenkins, who concealed their avarice under the cloak of humanitarian aid: "Yes," said Bonaparte, "I had money, I had lands, I said to my wife, 'There is Africa, a struggling country; they want capital; they want men of talent; they want men of ability to open up that land. Let us go.' " (p. 54) England was in the process of becoming what Schreiner called an "inchoate trading firm" (TSA, 50) in South Africa during her formative years, and Blenkins represents the most disreputable face of imperialism.

Bonaparte's attempt at a total takeover of the farm, after ousting Otto from favor and destroying the hope of intellectual and scientific advance promised by Waldo, represents the calculating economic exploitation that was about to be ushered in when the novel opens, in 1858, and that would eventually precipitate the Anglo-Boer war of 1899–1902.[4] Industrialization, which could have been managed by new indigenous resources, such as Waldo's sheep-shearing machine, would take the form of invasion by a ragged crowd of immoral fortune hunters from all over the world. The contest over the mineral resources—diamonds and gold—found in the seventies and eighties in the Orange Free State and the Transvaal would be expressed in terms of Boer republicanism and British imperialism. Rumors of diamond wealth had circulated since the early sixties; the first sizable diamond was found in 1867 (at the opening of chapter 2 Lyndall and Em discuss diamonds and the "crystals" they have picked up; later Lyndall flashes an expensive diamond ring). In October 1871 the fields were proclaimed British territory under the name Griqualand West, and in 1873, while Schreiner was there, they became a crown colony under a lieutenant governor. Also at this time, New Rush was named as the colony's capital. The aspirations of the cluster of colonial children are played out against these tensions between Boer control and British imperialism: a struggle over the control of indigenous wealth. In this struggle the indigenous African people, the first diamond hunters, were elbowed aside and became "a shrinking minority" (Schoeman, 259). Here Cecil Rhodes, later Schreiner's enemy as the prime representative of British capitalism in South Africa, began to build up his fortunes.

Here the future shape of the mining industry, which would in turn determine the country's political future and its notorious legislation of migrant labor and racial difference, was laid down. The phases and motives of imperialism in Africa are graphically and satirically presented in the first part of the novel in the attempted coup by Bonaparte Blenkins, his vanquishing of old Otto, and his more difficult, ultimately unsuccessful struggle with the Boer Tant Sannie. The renting of half the farm to the "new man," effete Gregory Rose, introduces us to another type of English settler/farm manager: Rose is an overrefined English colonial who, like Blenkins, can reinvent his family history in a more pleasing and pretentious form and who, like Blenkins, is undone by courting one woman while still apparently courting another. In Blenkins's struggle to control the farm, the superstition of Boer Christianity is strongly linked with the hypocrisy of imperialism in the alliance of Blenkins and Tant Sannie. The censorship later notoriously related to the South African state had one significant result: "Whenever you come into contact with any book, person, or opinion of which you absolutely comprehend nothing, declare that book, person, or opinion to be immoral. . . . Do all that in you lies to annihilate that book, person, or opinion" (p. 104). Another result of this alliance is that brute force is used to control others: Waldo is tied up and beaten; the girls are locked in and punished. The adult-child relationship, where superior size and force almost always prevail, is a prototype for all other abuses of power. This is the case particularly in South Africa, where the power to wound, torture, and confine a majority labor force and keep them without a voice and rights, has been crucial and where paternalistic protection has been cited as justification.[5]

The chapter headings, satirically deploying religious texts ("I was a stranger, and ye took me in"; "Blessed is he that believeth") underline the exploitation that takes place under the cloak of religious respectability. Christian imperialists are represented as either holy fools or rogues. Fortunately, their African converts are shown to have their own resources and resilience: "[T]he boys winked at each other, and worked as slowly as they possibly could" (p. 32). These headings give way to others that figure Blenkins as both a rapacious animal and a hunter: "Bonaparte Blenkins makes his nest"; "He sets his trap"; "He catches the old bird"; "He shows his teeth"; "He snaps"; "He bites." Blenkins as a bird of prey is the human opposite of the "white bird of truth" that true questers seek, and the farm ostrich recognizes him as its legitimate target. Schreiner's concern with mouths, devouring, cannibalism, and avarice is extended from *Undine* and tied to an instinctive understanding of imperialism as a predatory process without compassion, tolerance, or respect for indigenous life forms. The sensitive intellectuals, first generation white

South Africans, the growing points of a possible new culture in the colony, are crushed; it could also be argued that they displace (and yet at another level represent) the indigenous people as the true victims of the colonizing process. As Jenny Sharpe argues of Brontë's *Jane Eyre*, there is in *African Farm* a keen self-consciousness of class and gender hierarchies, but "race operates as a transparent category of self-representation."[6] Schreiner's passionate sympathies lie with young creatures like herself—talented colonial children—and in her sense of their victimization. The indigenous Bantu people are merely sullen and ugly presences or creatures at one with the African land; the Hottentots become the accomplices of Boer authority and European invasion (pp. 44, 82) and the San people the traces of earlier cycles of oppression, sympathetic when they are artists. Nevertheless, the strong focus on South Africa as a site of oppression maintained by ignorant forces (Waldo becomes sullen and ugly under tyranny, too) has a wide range of reference. Schreiner herself occupied the position of domestic, exploited labor, later almost the exclusive position of black domestic servants in South Africa.

Schreiner said that the farcical figures of Tant Sannie and Bonaparte Blenkins were put in to balance the tragedy of Waldo and Lyndall, so she had an artistic sense of the balances and oppositions she wanted to construct in the novel, which is built on a pattern of repetition and variation, parallels and contrasts, at every level. Part 1 concerns the rise and fall of Bonaparte Blenkins, a farcical colonial replay of the European fortunes of Napoleon Bonaparte, who wanted to be "master of the world" (p. 40) as Bonaparte aims to be "master of this farm" (p. 94). Napoleon is invoked in an early discussion between the children and is admired by Lyndall for his single authority and his solitary martyrdom on the island of Saint Helena. Lyndall, a girl with a strong will and the only one to see through Bonaparte right away, identifies with Napoleon, his strong will, and his final martyrdom, exhibiting the empathy and imagination of the novelist who tells us what the "brown history" book never tells (p. 41): inner thoughts and consciousness. Part 1 is thus an absurd rendering of a power struggle on the farm that represents a tussle between European economic settlerdom and tenacious Boer authority over the land, a struggle during which the gentle, intelligent (white) children are beaten and crushed. African children are assimilated to nature, like the "small animal" who rolls around in the sawdust with the puppy at the opening of the last chapter, or the servants who are presented in a stereotypic way as comic if they are at all Europeanized: "the spruce Hottentot in a starched white 'kappje' and her husband on the other side of the door, with his wool oiled and very much combed out, and staring at his new leather boots" (p. 62). Less civilized natives, such as the "Kaffir herd" whom Lyndall describes as a "splendid fellow" (p. 213), is made the subject of Lyndall's evolutionary speculations, presented as part of a modern, rational worldview. Evolutionary thought marks the Victorian boundary that circumscribes the novel.[7]

The novel itself encompasses more than Lyndall's modern views. Waldo and Lyndall represent the gentleness, will, and intelligence of the New Man and Woman, oppressed by the brutality of material colonial conditions, which include Tant Sannie's superstitious ignorance and Blenkins's self-serving will to power. All the oppressed children can do is comfort each other that "we shall have the power too, some day" (p. 117), although this proves to be a false prophecy. The novel is a complex meditation on what it means to "have the power," on what is done with power, on how it is used and abused, and on different kinds of power: political, intellectual, imaginative. Part 2 seems to recognize that "having the power" in South Africa means occupying the unacceptable place of tyranny: As Graham Pechey points out, Waldo does not reach the Diamond Fields because he cannot condone the cruelty practiced as a means of getting there (Pechey, 17). The overreaching greed of Blenkins undoes him, and he is banished from the farm but not until a great deal of harm has been done. Part 2 would deal with the struggles and constrictions that are intrinsic to colonial life and that affect young (white) adults seeking love and meaningful work in society. The multiple ironies and disappointments of this process reveal an overriding pessimism of view that marks Schreiner as a late Victorian, a writer who has a romantic rebel as heroine, like Brontë's Jane Eyre. Nevertheless, her emphasis on renunciation and failure where "social and religious constraints are supreme and final arbiters" mark her as part of high Victorianism even as she dismantles the orthodoxies of religion and gender norms in her polemic and artistic method.[8]

In part 1 the scars and solitude of childhood are given memorable expression in a South African landscape, one not yet passionately rendered within representative fiction as "integral to events" and as "a force that touches (the characters') lives directly" (Schoeman, 436). As many critics have remarked, the strength of this founding South African fiction resides in its inversion of metropolis and colony, making the indigenous place the center of attention, the point of origin and return, and making the Europeans "strangers," invaders, and transients in this place, both locating and problematizing "the idea of home," center and margin.[9] African landscape is a source of desolation, consolation, and "oppressive beauty," a place where human communication is rare, where the only community rituals are those that rely on the exclusion of others and where intolerance is the norm.

Many of the patterns of behavior and circumstance that would be typical of young adulthood are anticipated in part 1. Waldo's gentle receptivity and his ultimate reabsorption into nature itself is prefigured when he lies under a rock in the first daylight scene and "a curious old ewe came to sniff at him" (p. 33). Em's passive role in her relationship with Gregory Rose is foreshadowed in her accepting attitude toward her surroundings: "God put the little 'kopje' here" (p. 42). Lyndall's tenacious will and rebellious anger are seen in a number of scenes with the other children and adults. We are shown her desire for wealth and fashionable attire as well as a hunger for knowledge and education. These desires reveal the divided consciousness of the New Woman, who wants intellectual autonomy but cannot renounce the desire for conventional feminine beauty and adornment. These patterns all bear out the burden of the epigraph: There is a continuity to character, shaped in the cradle, where ruling "prejudices," "habits," and "passions" are established. Thus the events and conflicts of part 1 are not just continuous with part 2, they are also causal. The experience of tyranny and cruelty in childhood shapes the children in different ways, leaving scars that affect adult relationships, making Em diffident, Waldo passive, and Lyndall angrily self-destructive (p. 120).

The two bridging sections between parts 1 and 2, sometimes called a diptych (Monsman 1991, 78), have been much criticized as unnecessary, irrelevant interpolations, or as too verbose and general. They do draw attention to the bipartite structure of the novel, however, and insert a very deliberate narrative pause between childhood and young adulthood, between farcical comedy and the lyrical gravity of part 2. They attempt to draw the general implications of the narrative together into a reflection on the phases of life itself, one beyond the differences of gender and individual character, and into an allegorical journey where the difficult lessons of struggle, suffering, and renunciation are formulated in another aesthetic key. "Times and Seasons" is a narrative dream inside Waldo's head as he lies on the red sand, a generalizing vision reconciling loss and healing, rooted to a real African earth; the Hunter allegory, as its title indicates ("Waldo's Stranger"), embodies the interpretation by a metropolitan outsider of an indigenous, primitive artwork, Waldo's carved gravepost for his father. Because "Times and Seasons" is typifying and integrative in mode—using the universalizing "we"—it becomes possible to reflect more fully on the implications of injustice for others: "The ox dies in the yoke, beneath its master's whip. . . . The black man is shot like a dog, and it goes well with the shooter" (p. 139). As Monsman points out, the narrative method transforms these experiences into "the common confession of both author and reader" (Monsman 1991, 78); this goes part of the way to rebutting the harsh critiques of Schreiner's vision as merely historically reflective.

Thus chapter 1 of part 2 is a movement toward a recognition of deep unity and coherence underlying and within the natural world, one located within a South African particularity: "[O]f that same exact shape and outline is our thorn-tree seen against the sky in midwinter: of that shape also is the delicate tracery between our rocks" (p. 142). An organic order linking human beings and nature is established as a peaceful point around which the chaos of experience turns and against which the jumbled social expectations of courtship and marriage, which follow, are placed in a larger context and revealed as the features of a particular time and place, which will change. The evolutionary perspective has the strength of a long view, invoking future change. This chapter is a foil for the search for revealed unitary truth in the Hunter allegory that follows, implying as it does that "truth" is all about us in the process of growth itself, found within time, not beyond it, as Lyndall will also recognize in her dying speech: "[G]reatness is to take the common things of life and walk truly among them" (p. 261). At the end of "Times and Seasons," "we walk in the great hall of life" (p. 143). The Hunter allegory reworks a different relationship between time, experience, and eternity, in a more tragic and pessimistic key and in a more formal allegorical mode. It uses the European mode of Christian allegory, secularized, and is offered to the indigenous artist Waldo, who can create a rough artwork but not interpret its meaning verbally. The context of the allegory, its articulation by a "decadent" stranger who despises Waldo's roughness, expresses a tension between Europe and Africa, sophistication and integrity, verbal facility and the dedicated ritual of a carving with a local, familial purpose. The allegory itself grows out of Otto's life journey, as "Times and Seasons" grows out of Waldo's, but both generalize about human life and an always frustrated quest for fulfillment and certainty. Both of these bridging sections deepen the tone and mood of the narrative in preparation for the movement of part 2 toward the deaths of Lyndall and Waldo, the two sacrificial lambs on the altar of modernity.

Part 2 is more closely concerned with social conditions and the gender norms that are inseparable from the processes of sexual partnership.

Here, Lyndall becomes a mouthpiece of feminist critique, for in her the complexities of contemporary courtship and marriage—and their separation from emotional honesty and personal fulfillment—are emphasized. Her schooling exemplifies the wholly inadequate way in which women were educated in the colonies. On the farm her first instructor is the ignorant schoolmaster, Blenkins; Lyndall then attends a small-town finishing school, from which she returns as a refined fashion plate (like the exquisite ideal displayed on Tant Sannie's wall). Intelligent, imaginative, and resourceful, she is offered nothing by way of real education or training for work in the world. In fact, the genteel womanhood forced upon her constricts her potential. Yet her steely hands on the reins and her forceful opposition to falsehood and tyranny reveal her as more capable of doing a "man's" work and more equipped for leadership than either Waldo or Gregory Rose. Her long, stirring feminist speech to Waldo (part 2, chapter 4) reveals that she has understood all of this: how women are reared for genteel wifehood and subordination to men and how they learn to achieve their aims through indirection and coquettish behavior. Despite this awareness, she feels unable to do anything to alter the status quo. Like Schreiner in her self-mistrust, she feels she will not attain release until she is loved by some noble man stronger than herself. Her incapacity to love—indeed, to feel much warmth at all—is mentioned. Her behavior toward her lover, who is also the father of her child, seems paradoxically self-defeating, although it illuminates the terms of contemporary marriage. She tries to control the marriage partnership by considering an empty marriage to a weak man who is devoted to her, Gregory Rose, ruthlessly appropriating him from his engagement to Em; she then behaves alternately like a needy child and a selfish woman toward her lover, who is presented, like Albert Blair, as attractive but arrogant. After her eloquence to Waldo and her plan to become an actress, for which she has the talent, she makes a destructive bargain with her "stranger," who is nameless. In the end, she is cared for by Gregory, transformed by a woman's disguise into a nurse, after her baby's death and shortly before her own. This destructive concatenation of events takes place as the carts sweep by to the diamond fields and a new South Africa is being born. The masculine Lyndall is reduced to a frail and wasted heap of muslin, the emphasis on clothing underlining her infantilization within feminine roles. Men, on the other hand, can be redeemed from conventional masculinity, as Gregory Rose is, only by living as women and substituting chastity and a serving love for a possessive control of women.

The scene in which Rose divests himself of masculine apparel and beard while in an African riverbed—the bedrock of his new identity—is vivid and curiously moving, as if sexual passion itself has to be dismantled before women and men can approach each other with an understanding of human need:

> So the horses changed masters, and Gregory walked off with his saddle-bags slung across his arm. Once out of sight of the waggons he struck out of the road and walked across the "veld," the dry, flowering grasses waving everywhere about him; halfway across the plain he came to a deep gully which the rain torrents had washed out, but which was now dry. Gregory sprang down into its red bed. It was a safe place, and quiet. . . . At his feet the dusty ants ran about, and the high red bank before him was covered by a network of roots and fibres washed bare by the rains. Above his head rose the clear blue African sky; at his side were the saddle-bags full of woman's clothing. (pp. 251–52)

This passage, with its anchoring of a modern psychosexual condition in the closely observed African setting, at once realistic and suggestive of Gregory's unconscious desires, is typical of the novel's ability to work on several levels at once with complex evocative effects. Sexual identity is revealed as fluid, a point made in many other ways in the novel, whereas gender norms are shown to be rigid. Schreiner constantly told Havelock Ellis, during their initial abortive romance, that passion separated her from him; she also struggled to maintain a partnership of working equals with mathematician Karl Pearson, even though it was finally overthrown by her needs as a woman. Her letters reveal constant reflections on possible ways of combining friendship and passion, but a realization that imbalances within contemporary marriage destroyed the basis for equality and thus for love. These insights are more than contemporary critique; they constitute a moving examination of sexual identity and the basis for any heterosexual partnership. Gregory's devoted nursing of Lyndall stands in contrast to the convenient social contract of Tant Sannie's wedding and the sexual instinct that draws Lyndall to her "stranger."

In the disjunction between Lyndall's speeches and her actions, the ambivalent position of the novel as one that simultaneously subverts and colludes with patriarchal norms and novelistic conventions is made most apparent. The way in which Lyndall's polemic threatens to take over the story points to a burgeoning feminist consciousness that is hard to confine within the novel; it is also a point at which the personal

authorial voice of a woman seems to intrude most, the voice that
inscribes feminist consciousness most directly and that has been most
appealing to women readers. Speaking from the heart, from painful
experience crystallizing into urgently felt metaphors and analogies, Lyndall's speech is a founding moment in women's fiction, opening up, as
Waldo recognizes, a "world of passion and feeling wholly new" (p. 178),
as well as a reminder of the hybrid art of the novel and Schreiner's consciously experimental breaking down of genre boundaries.[10] Lyndall's
speech reveals that *African Farm* is also a narrative of ideas, a "problem
novel." As Pechey points out, part 2 of the novel consists mainly of
monologues, some narrated and some written as letters (like Waldo's
letter to the dead Lyndall). This proliferation of different sustained
voices gives various characters the space to tell their story from their
own point of view, resisting in its polyphony any totalizing narrative
control. The hybrid art of *African Farm* thus resists both the male adventure narrative with its focus on external, "conquering" events and any
novelistic discourse that constrains its characters within the iron laws of
probability and naturalistic convention. Here, as in other respects, the
novel is a paradigm of the relational sympathy and tolerance of diversity
it advocates as antidotes to rule by force.

Em is both a foil to Lyndall and differently related to colonial power.
She inherits the farm after Tant Sannie's wedding takes her off to
another farm. Em's link with the land and a form of colonial continuity
is emphasized in her songs and her listening, patient receptivity as first
Gregory and then Waldo, chastened by their unhappy times away from
the farm, return to tell their stories. The farm has become a gentler
place with this generation; the parlor has been opened and has taken on
a "bright habitable aspect" (p. 207), but the marriage that will inhabit it
has been emptied by Gregory's betrayal. Once again, the form of marriage is separated from the vital love that should give it meaning. All of
the considered or actual marriages are compromised or worthless, thus
dramatizing Schreiner's belief that for the best men and women of her
day marriage would have to be forfeited or deferred. As she herself
explained, *African Farm* did not propose that marriage was unnecessary,
rather that it should not be accepted on any but the highest terms.
Deferral becomes the condition of ideal value: True marriage, like the
true woman, is "yet a dream of the future" (Parkins-Goumelas, 46–47).

African Farm thus charts the high expectations, disappointments, and
deaths of the two main protagonists, Lyndall and Waldo, and the compromised survival of Gregory and Em. The opposite sexes, but inverted

gender traits, of Waldo and Lyndall, allow a complex commentary on gender norms, colonial possibilities, and constriction. Waldo's quest for meaningful work ends when an act of extreme brutality forces his intervention between transport driver and his beaten black ox (a much reiterated trope in South African fiction for arbitrary violence, like the crimes committed against African people). Waldo is marginal because his gentle philosophical nature makes him ill suited to the acquisitive role of businessman; constant menial labor is shown as destructive of all finer instincts and of thought itself. Lyndall's ambitions are destroyed by a complex bind of sexual morality, personal need, and social norms. Those who inherit the land are without passionate striving or high aims; those who die carry the burden of consciousness and intellect with them. *African Farm*, as Schreiner saw it, is a kind of African *Romeo and Juliet* in which the contentious forces of colonialism destroy two young and talented people before they have reached fruition. The future portended by the brutality or passivity of the survivors in South Africa was accurate enough, so was the portrayal of the religious and social norms that cut in upon individual identity.

At the same time, an organic unity suggested by this artistic simulacrum, the novel itself, and the mystical moments of rest and self-integration found within it by Lyndall and Waldo at their deaths invokes a more profound and lasting order than that of society. This artistic form summons up a peaceful simultaneity that counters the abuse of power inherent in patriarchy, colonialism, and an emergent industrialism, where body is always bruised to pleasure soul. The novel abounds in artistic analogues: Waldo's gravepost and carved box, Lyndall's depiction of the empathetic aspects of acting, Waldo's contemplation of the organic harmony at the farm pigsty, all work strongly to suggest ways in which the human imagination constantly feeds on and transforms the data of experience into living wholes, despite the discontinuities of experience. The manifold narrative forms of the novel—dreams, songs, letters, sermons, lies, parodies of contemporary prose styles (such as the hunter's tale and the colonial romance)—reveal how language itself constructs meaning through parody and self-referentiality. Everyone has a different story to tell and tells it differently, with more or less eloquence and more or less truthfulness. The narrative sets up complex, individual relationships with truth that simultaneously reveal truth as a function of quest, journey, and process. "And that too has its truth," we are told (p. 266). Lies, self-delusions, fantasies, day- and nighttime dreams exist on a complex continuum. Dream life and real life are sometimes hard to distinguish but are held, without being constrained, within the controlling dream of the overall narrative, which yields to doubt at any moment of closure. There is a constant commentary on art and aesthetic response, reception, critical commentary, publication, various tales and tellers. Art "says more than it says, and takes you away from itself. It is a little door that opens into an infinite hall where you may find what you please. . . . it will yet find interpreters" (p. 157). Art is also what lets us "out" of the iron walls of individual life, through the empathy between author and characters, or between readers, characters, and author, imagined and historical lives that intersect in the processes of creation and reception.

Gendered polarities are also questioned and dissolved at a number of levels: in the duet of masculine Lyndall and feminine Gregory Rose (Parkins-Goumelas, 103) and at another level within the textually constructed androgynous author, Olive Schreiner, impersonating Ralph Iron, who originally signed the novel as author (Monsman, 106–7). If women writers had to impersonate men in order to get published at all and maintain their female decorum, they were equipped with a full understanding of the need for masks and false male names in order to enter a domain of authorship marked as male. Gender duality is inscribed on the title page history of *African Farm*, with its virile and strong pen name and its later loving, feminine inscription to a female friend. This duality of address suggests a dichotomy within the creative consciousness of the "author," so that gender is also deconstructed at the level of authorship and textuality. The controlling narrative voice, at times extracting the general laws of behavior and morality in a time-honored male tradition of lawgiver and omniscient patriarch, at times fusing with a passionate young woman's protest at the conditions of women's lives, is without gender.

The novel is called *The Story of an African Farm*, as though it is the farm that speaks, and in a sense this is true. The farm landscape itself seems to have a deeper memory than any of the characters (pp. 195, 212). The human beings are surrounded and partly dwarfed by the land; parcels of the land are held by farmers, but such patrilineal systems do not benefit the orphans Lyndall and Waldo, whose orphanhood is symbolic of their marginality in the colony. The process by which a mystical moment within an isolated African landscape reconnects Waldo with an intuited order and harmony within nature suggests that for the disinherited colonial the imaginative response to indigenous nature replaces any actual control over the land. Feminist protest is only one of the voices within the novel, but it is a powerful one, suggesting that the colonial order is largely man made, according to male norms that reduce women (Em as much as Lyndall) to the status of adornments or possessions. The emergence of Em as farm-owner, however, presages a similar moment toward the end of *From Man to Man*, when Rebekah buys a small farm of her own. Thus the economic basis of female autonomy is suggested, in keeping with Schreiner's feminism elsewhere. Although the Hottentot servants and the Kaffir herdsman are seen as creatures on a lower evolutionary rung or as complicit with Boer farmers, the narrative as a whole is a commentary on patterns and cycles of invasion and dispossession that rely on brute force and a crushing of the generosity or compassion that might undergird a new political order. Thus it predicts the future of the South African state while showing the nature of any colonizing process, resting as it does on hypocrisy, exploitation, and domination by superior force. "Story" can only partly transform and heal "history," but it does suggest alternatives to entrenched patterns of domination.

Only certain forms of narrative and discourse were historically available to articulate these alternatives, and Schreiner shows herself keenly aware of how she needed to reshape the novel pattern she knew in order to express the truths of an African farm as she knew it. In particular, she perceived a need to spiritualize the novel, to dwell on different inner consciousnesses, to put existential struggle at the center, and to show what people thought as well as what they did. She also believed it was necessary to challenge through mockery and irony the dominant discourses that made only the exotic, the physical adventures of a male group, and the conventionally respectable into the stuff of fiction. *African Farm* is an experimental novel that anticipates modernist experimentation with voice, consciousness, and structure: "Times and Seasons" anticipates Virginia Woolf's "Time Passes" in *To the Lighthouse* (Bjordhove, 52); the cyclical, lyrical patterning of childhood moments in time anticipates the work of Katherine Mansfield; in both cases *African Farm* may well have been a shaping influence.[11] In particular, the organization of the novel according to symbolic moments and organic feminism was bravely experimental and a forerunner of many novels to follow. In allowing the personal disappointments and the conflicts between sexual need and social conformity experienced by women to be given such play, Schreiner anticipated a host of subsequent novels by women in which sexual politics becomes central. These included the directly influenced Doris Lessing, South African writers such as Bessie Head[12] and Nadine Gordimer, and other creators of feminist writings such

as Margaret Laurence, Fay Weldon, Margaret Atwood, and Margaret
Drabble—writers who collapse the boundary between popular and serious fiction and who use the personal, domestic dramas of women's lives
as an index to the health of society and human development. Schreiner's
famous novel initiated a South African postcolonial protest linked with
feminist critique.

In *African Farm* Schreiner found a form that suited her drive toward
articulating many selves, many possibilities, including those not fixed by
gender or orthodoxy, while showing all of these possibilities as natural
outgrowths of a South African colony at a particular point in time,
where industrialization was about to oust older rural lifestyles and customs and where a new phase of European imperialism was about to
begin. The scene of the "Boer wedding" (part 11, chapter 6), held in the
stillness of a dusty daguerreotype, symbolizes a fading order. The manner in which Schreiner's novel indigenizes or incorporates European genres such as the novel and allegory invokes both Africa and Europe, suggesting some ways in which they are inextricably mixed and others in
which they would always be mutually incomprehensible. *African Farm*
continues to stand on a bridge between European and African audiences, to each of which the other's home is alien. The journeys of
Schreiner's fiction are as circular as her life journeys, showing the difficulty of a divided English colonial consciousness as well as the fragmented aims of a modern woman trying to earn a living by writing. The
rich rendering of many languages and dialects in *African Farm* as well as
many forms of silence and misunderstanding suggests that language
both constitutes the realities we know and is inadequate to render our
experiences fully. Although there is great emphasis in the novel on solitary suffering and solitude, moments of consolation can be found in
company, typically in an act of communication to a sympathetic listener
("Perhaps it was a relief to him to speak" p. 247) or in the peaceful solitude found within African nature where nature itself is shaken into communication: "There was one among the trees on the bank that stood out
against the white sky. All the other trees were silent; but this one shook
and trembled against the sky. Everything else was still; but those leaves
were quivering, quivering. I stood on the sand; I could not go away.
When it was quite dark, and the stars had come, I crept out" (p. 244).

This scene marks Waldo's return to the African farm he left for the
wider challenge of work in the world and on which he will die in the
sunshine on a "princely day." Time and eternity are strongly compressed
within such moments in the narrative. Like the hunter in the allegory,

Waldo does not die comfortless. One feather, especially if it is the quill of the writer, is enough to construe the whole bird. Final meanings are deferred and left open to further question. The novel *African Farm* is both communicative and enigmatic, like the farm itself. By telling its story as truly as she could, Schreiner told her readers more than she knew about its past and future and etched compelling images of the forms of freedom and constraint that were operative in the present and would partly determine the future.

Chapter Four

Sisterhood Is Powerful:
From Man to Man

The incompleteness of *From Man to Man*, posthumously published in 1926 by Schreiner's husband, S. C. Cronwright-Schreiner, is only one of the critical problems associated with this moving, impassioned, bulky work-in-progress, the "big novel" redolent with the incompleteness of life itself. The origins of the novel are complex, the novel representing many strata of Schreiner's life experience and phases of reflection on that experience, including the changing history of South Africa and her shifting residence outside and within the country. The novel was begun quite early, during the same period as *The Story of an African Farm*, and seems to have been conceived as a fuller portrait of the "fallen woman," and a broader representation of the psychological consequences of sexual transgression in a conservative, Puritanical colonial town, especially the sense of being hounded by scandalmongers. That Schreiner herself suffered from a deep sense of shame and persecution following the Gau affair is evident in a few anguished outbursts in her letters many years after the relationship had ended. Bertie's story, that of a "simple, child-like woman, that goes down, down" (Rive, *Letters,* 38), would be the carrier of these negative life experiences. It is the tale of a sensual, innocent woman who has few intellectual resources or defenses against men or social judgments. (Bertie is both a diminutive of a masculine name and of one of Schreiner's given names, Albertina; it is also the female counterpart to the exploitative male hero of *Undine*, Albert Blair.)

After apparently submitting the manuscript to Chapman and Hall in 1881, complete in an early form and before her submission of *The Story of an African Farm*, Schreiner decided to extensively revise the novel, destroying the integrity of the early version and unable to find a satisfactory form for the new one. She wrote to Ellis: "You see, dear one, I have so cut up and changed the thing that there is hardly anything left, and I don't know how to put it together. . . . I think it was the Devil made me unpick it" (Draznin, 90–91). Ellis suggested to her that she should simply finish it according to her original conception, but this was not possible. She left the novel for very long periods of time, although she worked at it sporadically in England, usually recasting and condensing the earlier version, and wrote the prelude in 1888. Back in South Africa much later, she also wrote some revisions and several new chapters. The novel became a storehouse for responses and ideas concerning women, marriage, social norms and racial justice, and a vehicle for feminist protest. But it also remained a story about two sisters, Rebekah and Bertie, one of whom marries and the other who is gradually degraded to the level of a prostitute, losing all will and self-possession and eventually becoming a pawn of others, especially men who "buy" her sexually and control her life.

Rebekah, the intellectual sister (carrying the name of Schreiner's intellectual and strong-willed mother), lives out the fate of a colonial wife and mother whose husband is unfaithful and whom she eventually forces into a separation agreement while keeping up the social veneer of marriage. The fates of the two sisters are contrasted but related, showing the two faces of Victorian women's fate, whether married or single, and suggesting that they spring from the same source, the distorted social view of women that reveres them as pure Madonnas but treats them as inferiors and sexual commodities. Both Bertie and Rebekah are viewed as desirable property when virginal and unmarried; both lose their value after seduction and marriage. The double standard benefits men and disadvantages both spinsters and wives. It sets women against one another in envy and sexual competition. The woman who gives her virginity before marriage loses her bargaining power and her reputation; all she can do is compound her original mistake and lose all sense of her own value or remain absolutely silent, as everyone advises her, horrified by her truthfulness. Within marriage, the wife who protests against her husband's infidelity finds that society not only condones it but even finds it normal and laudable. Women are tarnished by sexuality and become objects of malicious gossip. A wife who is also a mother has very few forms of redress other than divorce, which would cause further scandal in such circles and deprive her children of a father.

These issues are richly articulated within a South African context in *From Man to Man.* The setting has grown to resemble a later South Africa, where the life of Cape Town, with a more established colonial society and social life, is added to the depiction of a farm childhood. *From Man to Man* is an attempt to chart in fiction the adult lives of colonial women, suggesting the terms available for relationships, the rocky shores of marriage as conventionally understood, and the degradation of sexuality outside marriage. Although it might have become a truism at the time that prostitution and marriage were two sides of the same coin, pointing to the materialistic nature of both transactions and the duality of image that affected women, *From Man to Man* is richly embedded in Victorian colonial landscapes: the Karoo farm, the upcountry town (Cradock), the Cape Town ballroom and salon, Muizenberg beach, and the Rondebosch suburban home. Seduction and adultery are given a local habitation and a name so that the characters come achingly alive, and the fauna and flora of the eastern Cape are lovingly realized in the indigenous settings. The pain of a woman discovering her husband's infidelity is given vivid and lengthy expression. Rebekah's very long letter to her husband ("that letter that you called a book," *FMM*, 304), replacing Lyndall's speech to Waldo, shows how explicit suffering supersedes the generalities of feminist rhetoric. It also depicts how willing Schreiner still is, as novelist, to stretch the fabric of the novel to accommodate the voice of personal female passion against injustice. One surmises that the protest was sanctioned and developed by Schreiner's own experience of marriage, for which there is some evidence, despite the early origins of the two sisters' narratives, but Rebekah's letter and her pain are also representative, speaking for and to other women, then and now. Some of the most graphic images are generated by the injury caused by sexual infidelity within marriage: "The time was long past when any mention of Mrs. Drummond affected her as rough matter touching a naked nerve-point; she had no living interest in her. But no creature which has ever crept into the core of our life, and fed on the bleeding macerated tissue it has created there, ever becomes for us again a matter of complete indifference. Anything connected with them makes in us a faint adumbration of pain" (p. 447).

In *African Farm*, the Hunter allegory appears as an almost detachable segment of narrative and has lent itself to separate publication. "The Child's Day"—the prelude of *From Man to Man*—was also separately conceived and written, although with an obvious organic relationship to the novel that follows, "The Woman's Day." One day in Alassio in 1888, Schreiner realized to her amazement "that it's a picture in small, a kind of allegory, of the life of the woman in the book!" (SCCS, *Letters,* 291). This conception of the prelude suggests that it sprang from the unconscious area of Schreiner's mind where *From Man to Man* continued to simmer as an unfinished creative work, spinning its own slow webs of further incidents and scenes. The prelude, echoing Wordsworth's *Prelude* in its charting of the growth of the creative mind in childhood, provides a metanarrative of female relatedness and separateness, nature and culture, in the childhood relationship of sisters. It was, in Schreiner's judgment and that of others, one of the finest things she ever wrote. She sent it to all of her closest friends: It was both a distillation of her own childhood ("real, about myself") and "a made up thing, an allegory of the life of the woman in the book." (SCCS, *Letters,* 291). The prelude charts a day in the life of the five-year-old Rebekah as she moves about the farm and inside the farmhouse on the day her mother gives birth to twin girls, one of whom dies (like the adults Bertie and Rebekah). This twinning image is a powerful organic figure for the lives of the two sisters that will apparently diverge greatly in adulthood. It also suggests that opposite life patterns can spring from the same cell, as is sometimes the case with twins. It opposes and interweaves images of biology and nurture. After Rebekah's initial jealous rejection of the new baby, the prelude shows her becoming a "little mother" as she adopts the stillborn child that has been put into the spare room and brings it ritualistic gifts; much later she returns to the main bedroom and lies down with her newborn sister in a position that suggests both motherhood and sisterhood: "But when [the mother] turned down the cover she found the hands of the sisters so interlocked, and the arm of the elder sister so closely round the younger, that she could not remove it without awaking both" (p. 73). These images powerfully suggest that damage done to one woman affects all women and that one of the richest sources of our social understanding is found within sibling relationships and the family. Schreiner's final dedication of the novel was to her dead little sister and her own stillborn daughter.

The prelude also shows that rituals, fantasy interludes, and role playing are effective ways in which to approach the world of action and take on roles that may seem difficult and unacceptable at first[1]. Rebekah is shown rehearsing motherhood with many make-believe babies. Her gifts to the dead twin combine African objects ("the Bushman stone") and English ones ("Queen Victoria's head"). "This one is mine," she says in protest when chased away from the dead child (p. 42); in the fantasy house she creates, she also has her own microscope, the father's object, "but this one was hers" (p. 46). In her fantasy interlude, she sees a "snow-white pod, nearly as long as her arm" (p. 47), which reveals a small baby, which she removes after breaking the string. This make-believe baby she comforts, tells stories, and nurses, all of her activities revealing the ways in which she has experienced her own childhood as a "strange child" who is different from others in her intellectual

precocity, willfulness, and storytelling. During the story fearful animals
are revealed as nonthreatening friends, females become heroines, and
Rebekah confesses to being an author herself. In the real world of play
afterward, Rebekah becomes a builder, like the men on the farm (and as
she will be as an adult). In childhood, all roles are possible in play,
although the voice of the scolding Ayah, representing household standards of conventional ladylike behavior, keeps breaking into Rebekah's
reveries and games. When Rebekah stages a tantrum to be allowed to
hold the live baby, she sobs: "[T]he long vibrating movement still went
on; it was almost as if a man were crying" (p. 72). Rebekah is established
as a masculine counterpart to her younger sister, a role that anticipates
her much later reverie when she imagines herself as a husband embrac-
ing a pregnant wife (p. 226). When Rebekah is suddenly confronted
with a real cobra after the imaginary one, she is both a frightened little
girl and somehow a participant in the snake's life: "[I]t was almost as if
she herself were a snake, and had gone krinkle! krinkle! krinkle! over
the grass" (p. 62). The empathetic imagination of the young writer is
always in evidence, flowing into forms of existence classified and separated by the adult world. Before she enters her mother's room, she
becomes interested in candlelight and shadows and conducts a small
experiment in which scientific curiosity gives way to faith and doubt:
"Perhaps only God knew what lights and shadows were" (p. 67). The
whole prelude is a skillful interweaving of dream and reality, rationality
and imagination, a vivid imagining of a child's day, presenting intuitive
apprehension as a real form of knowledge. It also shows behavior as both
propensity and reaction, growth as a utilization of fantasy in the service
of familial and social relationships, and the imagination as a map of reality that can become reality. In this process, some of the binaries set up in
critical thought, including feminism, are collapsed. The biological and
cultural are shown as inseparable, richly interwoven, as both experience
and the construction of experience. Writing of the prelude, especially its
"multiple allegorical registers," Laura Donaldson suggests that it provides a metanarrative for contemporary feminism, problematizing "a
radical politics of identity" (p. 132) while indicating that the basis of any
feminist position turns on experience as well as on the cultural construction of experience[2]. In the rich interplay of imagination and reality, a
little girl can occupy the place of an adult man and woman and thus
know what it is like to be of different sexes; she can also know in an
instant what the small procession of men with spades across the farm
meant (burial and death), and that sudden burst of knowledge can in

turn inform her of the nature of childbirth and adult sexuality: "[S]he would never again look for a new little baby, or expect to find it anywhere; vaguely but quite certainly something of its genesis had flashed on her" (p. 64).

Like Katherine Mansfield's short story "Prelude," with which it bears comparison, and like Saul Bellow's similar, lyrical *Seize the Day,* the prelude takes up only one day of a life and yet contains the seeds of life and death and of adult life in society. It uses the cycle of the day as an allegory of the life-learning process, especially for women and even more so for the artist in whom imagination and intuition are highly developed. It seems to follow the movements of the mind itself as it apprehends, imagines, and makes new combinations of dreams and real life. The prelude is also an implicit meditation on the relationship of metropolis and colony, big and little islands, large and small Queen Victorias, and real and imaginative kingdoms. Once again the metropolis/colony relationship is inverted, and the little Queen Victoria lays down the terms on which she will inhabit her "island" (as she will later state her terms to her faithless husband). Created in the image of her desires, her island, like her baby, is proportionate to her needs. In the real world of the Victorian Cape Colony, reality will keep intruding harshly on such desires and dreams, yet Rebekah will keep alive in adulthood the ideals and dreams of childhood, seeking to build on the fragments of reality a new order, or dream it into being and create the basis for a new sisterhood of women and a new comradeship in marriage. The prelude is thus a full portrait of the child as mother to the woman, both progenitor and microcosm of the adult woman, Rebekah, who will continue to bring the life of vision to bear on the real world, which will go on being resistant to transformation by vision.

The title of the novel—"The Woman's Day"—suggests that the novel, like the prelude, has a strong allegorical, representative dimension. It consists of the alternating stories of Rebekah and Bertie in adulthood, although one plan suggests that a third section, called "Rebekah," would have shown Rebekah as the new autonomous woman after Bertie's death. Bertie's story is of a decline into depression and increasing passivity. She is depicted as an inarticulate woman who is the repository of domestic virtue, a wonderful cook, seamstress, and housekeeper who would have been a fulfilled wife and mother under normal circumstances, as she lacks Rebekah's intellectual curiosity and aspiration to a wider world. Yet Bertie is the one destroyed by her own loving and honest nature after the initial seduction by her English tutor at the age of

15. She recovers from the seduction itself but cannot recover from the loss of John-Ferdinand, the suitor whom she loves and to whom she tells the truth, nor from the malevolent gossip passed on by Veronica Grey, the Englishwoman who first destroys Bertie's photographic image and insistently takes her place as John-Ferdinand's wife and then persecutes her with gossip. Veronica is a successful female version of Bonaparte Blenkins and a chilling picture of psychological substitution by which she becomes mistress of an African farm, then a serene wife and mother.

Bertie's graphically rendered sense of persecution, which seems to predate the events of her adolescence in childhood nightmares, and her childishness, encoded in her name, Baby-Bertie, leave her vulnerable to the world and propel her into apparently inexplicable flight whenever the shadow of gossip and disapproval fall over her again. She is shown as a mute, fearful woman, incapable of asserting herself or even overcoming her shame enough to enlist her sister's help. She feels shut out of the respectable world forever and is eventually forced by circumstance to accept the protection of a Jewish diamond buyer and go with him to England. The mercantilism of the Diamond Fields and the nascent capitalist system are thus linked with the "buying" of women. In England her increasing alienation from her surroundings and from herself are graphically rendered; moods and events suggest that Schreiner was drawing on her own first years in England, where she suffered a deep sense of loss of an earlier identity, was overwhelmed by the alien, shabby urban environment and climate of Victorian London, and disturbed by her own sexual responses to a man she called a "sadist" and who made her feel like a "prostitute"[3]. Bertie's narrative is a convincing portrait of the slide into depression and degradation that such a colonial woman in similar circumstances might undergo. Bertie's search for a piece of "country" in London, a landscape that she might be able to relate to by recalling South Africa, indicates the strong roots Schreiner herself had in South Africa and how well she understood the overthrow of self that a sudden loss of a cloistered, innocent farm childhood, of family, and of a known and loved colonial landscape, might mean. Bertie becomes the first exiled woman in South African literature. Rebekah is offered marriage by the other boy cousin, Frank, who is presented from the first as capable of cruelty and enjoying mastery over his animals as he later will over women. Although she loves Frank and responds to his courtship, a rift in their marriage widens as Rebekah's growing responsibilities as wife and mother of four children threaten to overwhelm her intellectual life. Hints of Frank's infidelity develop into the full-scale arraignment she sends him in a letter he refuses to read. Schreiner details Rebekah's deep sense of affront and betrayal as she has gradually discovered that Frank simply enjoys chasing and possessing other women, afterward despising them, while continuing to feel that his wife is the "Madonna," perfect mother, and convenient housekeeper, without any rights of her own. Rebekah's sense of disbelief, growing disillusionment, pain, and outrage are fully rendered in her letter, triggered by her most recent discovery that he has a sexual relationship with the Colored servant of the household. Rebekah adopts the child of this union, Sartje, although the mother disappears, presumably sent away by Rebekah. Schreiner intended these events to represent the historical creation of South Africa's mixed race ("Colored") population, and Rebekah's response to her husband's sexual appropriation of the servant (slave) would suggest a longsighted overcoming of the racial prejudice that has been inflicted on the Colored people. The fact that Sartje has a different status and is taught to call Rebekah "mistress" mitigates the liberal intentions behind this gesture as does the scornful depiction of the servant mistress in derogatory racial terms. Presented mainly through an allegory of a technologically superior white race arriving on earth and finding late Victorian civilization distinctly wanting, Rebekah's discourse on racial prejudice, however, is both innovative and ahead of its time despite its didacticism. These events allow Schreiner to link racism and sexism; she develops this modern insight in her essay called "The Problem of Slavery," in which she argues that slavery as an institution was "less at discord with the moral and intellectual condition of the Boer than are today at variance with our own those lineal descendants of slavery, the disabilities attaching to sex or class, which in our most civilized societies still exist" (*TSA*, 105). *From Man to Man* is a graphic depiction of these disabilities, and Rebekah, in another discursive interlude on the nature of human progress, evolution, and decadence (pp. 177–225), describes slavery as a "rotten foundation stone" for any society (p. 190). Rebekah's gesture is intended as exemplary in a society where the Colored people have been treated as only a useful resource for whites. The name of the child, as Tony Voss has pointed out, suggests that Schreiner is referring to the figure of Saartjie Baartman, the "Hottentot Venus" who was put on display in Europe[4]. Schreiner offers us a realistic portrait of a mixed-race family coping with social problems and prejudice, including the prejudice of Rebekah's white children, instead of the frontier myth that legitimated European ethnocentric unease.

The novel comprises four discursive "interpolations": Rebekah's "ideas" article, written one night (chapter 7); her long letter to Frank on adultery and marriage (chapter 8); her disquisition and allegory to her children concerning racial "superiority" (chapter 12, told while Frank has a long bath!); and the discussion between Rebekah and Drummond near the end of the manuscript (chapter 13) on art, writing, and the creative process. Each is cast in a different form and tone, and each has a bearing on the issues explored within the narratives. As Schreiner argues, they "are all point, if only someone will take the trouble to see the point" (SCCS, *Letters,* 100). The first essay is an exploration of the idea that remains implicit in *African Farm,* that the spirit of the modern age differs from the previous Christian era and repeats the classical urge to "know reality as it is," to uncover the facts scientifically rather than be handed arbitrary dogmas. Any censorship is opposed, the "habitual suppression in art of certain aspects of life," those aspects of women's life, for instance, that Rebekah's and Bertie's stories candidly reveal in this novel. In this meditation, which contests the implications of "the survival of the fittest" principle, truth is linked with art and science, and both are linked with an underlying principle of creative love, "the fount and core of life" (p. 214). Scientific knowledge unites all of life; true art puts us in touch with reality. This section illustrates Schreiner's self-consciousness as an emergent, modern voice, reflecting on the significance of contemporary consciousness. It also shows her reflecting on the nature of empires, decadence, the brute domination behind imperialism, and the composition of a just society. The subjection of women is one strand of the argument: Women of Greece did not share in the "culture and freedom and labors of its males" (p. 190). The notion of a wasted female talent equivalent to Shakespeare's but spending a life "brewing currant wine and making pastries" (p. 219, anticipating Virginia Woolf's "Shakespeare's sister" notion in *A Room of One's Own*) is illustrated by Rebekah's example of a strong intellect craving expression in the real world, but shut up with household routines and child rearing. A running motif in the novel, the statue of Hercules, links the classical and modern ages and the expression of truth in art. The statue passes from Drummond to Rebekah, who are both writers and have sympathetic intellectual interests and moral principles. This whole section moves toward a celebration of creative love as the mainspring of human progress and achievement, a life force that draws the living world together. It is a "moving original power" (p. 213) that opposes its powerful creative connection to the instinct for hunting, killing, and domination that links Frank to conventional masculine values. Imaginative kinship and empathy, the "line of connection" (p. 292) made by the imagination, is a core value for Schreiner, one she opposes to any form of domination, whether that of colonial conquest or masculine control. Her fiction is itself an example of this creative love, which spends itself "to produce that which gives infinite joy without ever being used up" (p. 214). Each of the abstract polemical sections advances this key argument a little further.

Rebekah's long letter to Frank extends some of these ideas in that infidelity is presented as a lived lie, destroying the truth on which a relationship should be based. It also serves as a revelation of the painfully constricted and humiliating life Rebekah has been living, which has been only hinted at before. Rebekah finds a new peace only when the sexual relationship between herself and Frank ceases, at her insistence. Sexuality is thus shown as the quicklime that keeps the bird in the cage, subjugates women, and perpetuates inequality (p. 306). This, too, anticipates many modern feminist arguments. The key to Rebekah's freedom is economic: Her ownership of a small farm and her readiness to work there and make it self-supporting free her from economic dependence on Frank.

The disquisition on race follows naturally on earlier discussion and events because it grows out of the consequences of Frank's sexual appropriation of a household servant and Rebekah's adoption of the child of that union. It also predicts future changes in racial attitude if children are educated by liberal mothers like Rebekah. The last discussion—on art and the stages of creative work—offers keen insights into Schreiner's independent thinking about the involuntary and voluntary elements in artistic creation and the role and position of the artist in society and humanity. Like Waldo's carving, these formulations bear "signs of patient thought" (*SAF*, 146). This discussion on the veranda simultaneously suggests that the true basis of a shared life for men and women is the close mental kinship seen at work in Rebekah and Drummond. The relationship is based on Schreiner's ideal, an intellectual sharing so close that sex itself falls away, as in the "third Heaven" of her allegory, "The Sunlight Lay" (she said the three stages of this allegory were in *From Man to Man* in objective form). Rebekah and Drummond together are an image of achieved androgyny, like the narrative consciousness of Ralph Iron in *African Farm*. They are almost interchangeable, as suggested by their similar hands, and the fact that Drummond is not only a writer but one who has an allegory suddenly occur to him just as

Schreiner's own prelude did (p. 467). He is not only Schreiner's male self incarnate but also "the New Man," her ideal of the caring, empathetic, nurturing male. The fact that he is the one who goes on the exploration of central Africa, which she always longed to do, reveals that she still felt that the world of action and exploration was possible only for men.

There were various projected endings for *From Man to Man*, told to different people at different times of her life, while the novel was still in process. They suggest that Bertie would die a degraded death, but Rebekah would envision at her death the fuller lives of the women of the future. Rebekah would not marry Drummond, feeling bound by the ties of morality and principle to care for her children and renounce personal fulfillment, but there would be a poignant parting scene between them. The novel as it stands almost suggests completion, being in its shape an exact fictional counterpart to the statue of the Winged Victory discussed by Rebekah, "without a head, without an arm, smitten and ill-treated, it would still stand the embodiment of Victory, calling men and women to struggle and conquer, though only through its broken fragment" (p. 469).

From Man to Man, Schreiner's posited title, implied the crucial value of charity to others, but other meanings are hinted at in the narratives themselves. They suggest that women's lives are controlled by the kinship system in which they are legally passed on from father to husband (like Rebekah, presided over by Queen Victoria and her consort). If this process is aborted by the woman's loss of virginity and marketable marriage value, she is passed from man to man as a degraded sexual object of exchange, as Bertie passes from the old Jew to his younger nephew (p. 400). Women have no value outside this kinship system and very little space outside the virgin/whore dichotomy. The fact that Rebekah's small study is maintained shows her attempt to maintain an autonomous intellectual life, and at least she is able to confront her husband and lay down her own terms for their future relationship, but the projected ending suggests that the social order still prevails against female self-fulfillment. Rebekah will not marry Drummond, nor will she travel to central Africa. The "camel-thorn," the title that actually appears on the manuscript, is a symbol of exploration reserved for men: "[H]e's been in Central Africa himself, and seen the great ant heaps and camel thorns" (p. 455). For women the "small bit of mimosa" that tears Bertie's dress as she runs down the path away from her shocked suitor evokes the way in which women are "torn" by small actions that are given overwhelming significance by a Puritanical society and by the gossip that destroys their

peace of mind. *From Man to Man* dismantles the interconnected privi-
leges of imperialism and patriarchy by revealing the immense damage
done to women by the replication of these structures and sites of power
within English-speaking colonial society.

Rebekah and Bertie, although physically separated throughout the
latter stages of the novel, are linked by their actual sisterhood, which,
like biological motherhood, works symbolically to evoke their different
but shared suffering as marginal creatures in a male owned and male
defined culture. They are linked in the implements with which they are
associated, the pen and the needle: "Has the pen or pencil dipped so
deep in the blood of the human race as the needle?" (p. 323) Rebekah's
pen stains her "little blue print skirt" as she walks up and down composing her ideas, suggesting that housekeeping and the life of a writer are
scarcely compatible. Moreover, the novel offers images of the woman
artist in the cave dweller who "took a bone from the heap from which
they had eaten and, with a sharp stone, began to carve on it those pictures and patterns which we find on the bones today . . ." (p. 425), a
female equivalent to Waldo's male San artist. The sisterhood of Bertie
and Rebekah is also socially symbolic of male control of women's sexuality and fertility: Bertie has no children and becomes the embodiment of
Schreiner's parasitic female; Rebekah, in her constant round of household and maternal activities after marriage, depicts the control of
woman's domestic labor and fertility within marriage. By adopting
Sartje, Rebekah breaks out of the pattern of legitimate patrilineal suc-
cession that controlled inheritance through male heirs.

From Man to Man is a closely woven fiction where everything—realistic narratives and dialogue, internal articles, letters, monologues, and
dialogues—has a bearing on everything else. The novel is closely and
sympathetically woven, and the characters are richly realized in their
South African or English settings. In particular, a line of indigenous veg-
etation delicately threads through the novel, weaving aloes and
plumbago, mimosas and avondbloem into lyrical evocation for the
organic life within nature that operates as a leading metaphor for the
desirable human ideal in society (pp. 438–39). From the wildflower
garden in the bush that is desecrated by Bertie's tutor, to the "little par-
lour" in the veld where Bertie is slowly courted by John-Ferdinand, to
Rebekah's suburban garden with its variety and profusion, organic
images suggest wrong and right relationships between nature and society, biology and culture. At the same time, a particular Eastern Province
landscape, recalling the Healdtown of Schreiner's childhood, is given a

rich and detailed fictional life (pp. 112–15). *From Man to Man* is also the first novel to show the particular memories and sufferings of a South African in exile, a banishment compounded by womanhood, bound within a patriarchy that is coextensive in colony and metropolis.

From Man to Man is closely tied to the developing insights of Schreiner's maturity and was meant to help other women by offering them images of the kinds of pain they would also have known from experience. The novel extends the biological image of motherhood into a principle of nurturing love that is related to the highest ideals of love, service, knowledge, and art and that is opposed to the drive toward physical domination and exploitation propelling imperialism and patriarchal power. At the same time, women's lives inside and outside the family, as then constituted, under the shadow of the ubiquitous portrait of Queen Victoria, are revealed as either stultifying of their potential or—worse—totally destructive of a woman's self-respect and identity. These were outspoken criticisms for the time. Although *From Man to Man* is a "womanly book," it also reveals that only insofar as women were able, like Rebekah, to escape the conventional constraints of gender, could they live at all. The life of personal relations that enclosed women could only partly satisfy, although the harmony between Rebekah and Drummond prefigures future possibilities, in which love might be based on a like-mindedness and equality. The novel made an end of Schreiner before she "made an end of it," but, in its courageous openness to her own evolving experience and knowledge, its very incompleteness is an index to the difficult transmutation of life into art.

From Man to Man fully reveals Schreiner's lifelong, dual commitment to the organic unfolding of individual life and a future society that might encourage that flowering for both sexes in a work of art "whose essential life and essence lie in its power of growth" (p. 221). If it is true that her characters embody aspects of her own personality and life, her experience of the conflicting responsibilities women like herself felt to the service of humanity and to art takes shape in Rebekah, whereas her vivid sense of the wounded, passive side of womanhood, a grief and loss beyond the reach of social reform, is given to Bertie. Yet the novel is impersonal, too: "[T]he artist is only an eye in the great human body, seeing for those who share (her) life" (p. 476).

From Man to Man represents Schreiner's "epic enterprise," one rooted in an experiential project to break open new ground in the depiction of intersecting forms of exploitation of women as the producers and reproducers of labor and to fictionalize a progressive movement toward new forms of companionship and "the reconstitution of community in South Africa" (Voss, 137, 144). Its long gestation allowed it to depict the emergence of a new historical juncture: "urbanization (and suburbanization), entrepreneurship, agency, and the complex indirect forces of bourgeois capitalism" (Voss, 143). At the same time, it revealed that in those more complex, mediated forms of bourgeois capitalism the control of women's labor and sexuality would still be the fulcrum of the bargain struck between metropolis and colony, capitalism and patriarchy[5]. The migration of women from homestead to city, colony to metropolis, could not be a liberating one until the "whole system" on which their lives rested was changed (Rive, *Letters,* 66). The story of Rebekah and Bertie is the story of two faces of womanhood in southern Africa at the transition from a precapitalist, rural society to a class-stratified, sex-gender system. Bertie, taken to London by a diamond buyer, symbolizes the mineral wealth of South Africa passing into foreign capitalist hands; Rebekah, struggling for forms of autonomy within colonial marriage, represents the power women had to reshape domestic space in order to resist and transform their own exploitation as units of domestic labor, reproducers of a patriarchal social order, and sexually betrayed keepers of the hearth. In reaching out to reshape gender norms, she perceived that they were intertwined with the racial norms that could be changed perhaps only by raising children to be the bearers of a new multiracial family and thus a new social order. This thesis anticipates the much later vision of Nadine Gordimer's 1981 novel, *July's People.*

From Man to Man, incomplete as it is, represents the furthest point to which the novel was capable of serving Schreiner's developing feminist vision of the lives of colonial women in South Africa. Its incompleteness is a graphic metaphor of the many contemporary lives shackled by patriarchy and racial prejudice. Schreiner would later turn to briefer and more immediate genres—allegory, pamphlets, and polemical nonfiction—to develop the insights and principles that she here attempted to manifest in the lives of her characters and double self, Rebekah and Bertie.

Chapter Five

The Dreamer as Reformer: *Dreams*

Allegory is a key to Schreiner's reformist vision and a master trope of her writing. As Gerald Monsman has argued, "the image of the artist as allegorist is central to Schreiner's aesthetics-as-politics, and her defense of allegory represents a highly sophisticated contribution to aesthetic, and perhaps political theory" (1992, 51). By remodeling allegory in her own terms, she secularized the religious typology of Bunyan and the tradition of Christian allegory and made it the vehicle of her critique of patriarchy, colonialism, and capitalism. Her allegories are both monumental and compressed, yet open to multiple interpretations. As in her definition of art, allegory "has a thousand meanings, and suggests a thousand more" (*SAF*, 157). This freedom of correspondence answered to her progressive social vision as it developed in the crucible of the 1880s in London, a decade rich in personal confusions and transformations, literary and cultural exchanges, friendships, sexual tension, and social life. Yet allegory had also been one of the formative tropes of her childhood training in biblical exegesis and of her visionary nonconformity. She had already used allegories as key components of the three novels written in Africa before 1881, drawing upon this mode as a resource to construct an "alternative configuration for the colonial suppression" of marginal lives "by an overwhelming cultural and technological power" (Monsman, 1992, 55). Thus the "Hunter allegory" she embedded in *The Story of an African Farm* symbolizes Waldo's quest in another mode, one that allows the significant elements of a historical struggle with the material conditions of nineteenth-century colonialism to be vividly portrayed and interlinked as part of a repeated human struggle to find meaning and value in life and to understand the moral basis of action in the world. The hunter represents the nature of metaphysical and ethical quest and dramatizes the need for a long view of human history. In such a concept, present renunciation, struggle, and suffering are needed so that the human race can progress to a higher condition, one in which companionship and love supersede the world of exploitation and violence created by colonial conquest, the patriarchal control of women, and the capitalist exploitation of labor. The hunter as metaphysical quester and worker replaces the imperial hunter, and allegory replaces, or stands in evocative contrast to, the male adventure tale of ravening lions and "hairsbreadth escapes," tales told by colonial opportunists like Bonaparte Blenkins. The quest for the truth stands in contrast to the great colonial lie that separates human beings from one another and stations them within a rigid hierarchy. Allegory, then, in Schreiner's case, is always about flux and process, a movement forward and upward by the quester, sometimes with a guide but often alone, across difficult and punishing terrain, a journey during which hard-won truths are wrung out by suffering. Although the allegories are open to multiple interpretations, they also dramatize a fundamental and binding truth that Schreiner saw as lying under "the socialist and humanitarian manifestations of our age," the important conception "of the unity and identity of Humanity (and of all things?)" that was "waking in our age" (Rive, *Letters*, 135). This conception of a binding brotherhood had been lacking in her South African experience and culture; in England she came in direct contact with a multifaceted movement toward new forms of human solidarity and equality and was deeply stirred by them. At the same time she had to find her own path to forms of expression that suited her vision, concerned as it was with the position of women within a hierarchically ordered society that was now being challenged and reconstituted.

Dreams was published in 1891, soon after Schreiner found herself back in South Africa after nine years in Europe. During those years she had struggled to establish herself as an independent woman and writer. Promising new relationships had ended in a renewed understanding that she could not marry and write and that passionate relationships with men led her into fear and rivalry, panic and flight. At the same time, the first half of the decade in London was full of intellectual stimulation, her own fame as author of *African Farm*, the comradeship of early socialist and progressive currents of thought and associations, debate, excitement, new publications by Hardy, Moore, Meredith, and Ibsen, and then a surge of interest toward France and the Symbolist movement, which she would finally allow to carry her out of England and away from Europe again—toward Africa.

The circumstances in England that led to her departure for South Africa in October 1889 and to the publication of *Dreams*, a watershed publication standing between England and South Africa (much like *African Farm* six years earlier), were complex, intertwining public and personal pressures. The sequence of allegories that she arranged and selected in *Dreams* was the crystallization of the thoughts and principles arising from the key experiences of the decade. Although she had a number of close friendships with women, chiefly Eleanor Marx and Alice Corthorn (the latter a struggling medical student she befriended and assisted), it was two relationships she had with men, both of whom would become prominent intellectuals in London, that would be crucial at this time. The first was with Havelock Ellis, an early admirer and reviewer of *African Farm,* with whom a loving friendship involving confession, closeness, cultural exchange, and experiments in passion soon developed. Ellis was in the medical training that Schreiner had proposed for herself when leaving South Africa for London and for which she found herself ill equipped and unsuited. He also passed on books and reviews to her; they shared their earlier colonial solitude (he had been in Australia) and key experiences and became each other's chief supports, confidants, and allies against the world. The letters reveal a relationship that became slightly suffocating when Ellis wanted a sexual relationship that was clearly not satisfying for Olive and that she felt destroyed the trust and friendship between them, breeding mistrust and possessiveness. He was her "other half," a family surrogate, a parent, a mirror image, a male twin, and a projection of the more active work she wanted to do in the world. The development of the relationship was a further illustration of her difficulty in combining sexual love and friendship, one of the topics of the allegories, which are much concerned with the problematic nature of male-female relationships, problems of jealousy, desire, exploitation, selflessness, autonomy, and the renunciation of desire.

Although at first a rich intellectual collaboration and dialogue, Schreiner's second relationship, with Karl Pearson, a mathematician (and after 1911, Galton Professor of eugenics) at University College, London, was much more destructive because it seemed for a while to hold out the promise of an ideal combination of passion and mental kinship and perhaps marriage and childbearing. A theme running throughout the allegories is the desire for a child, always held close to the breast, and the last, most difficult desire for the allegorized woman to renounce. Ironically, Schreiner met Pearson through the Men and Women's Club, which he founded in London in 1885 as a forum for new intellectual and scientific debates about sexuality, marriage, passion, prostitution, and friendship. As Judith Walkowitz has pointed out, the proliferating discourses about sexuality in London during the 1880s were both earnest and utopian and were conducted at a polite level that concealed another, darker discourse of desire and domination.[1] She also argues that there was a "dialectic between sexual possibility and sexual danger that reveals radically different attitudes toward masculinity and femininity, and especially heterosexuality, on the part of men and women" (p. 38).

Schreiner both contributed toward and struggled to define her own identity within these shifting and problematic definitions. The club discussions had an air of frankness; yet the women, especially, were fearful of losing their respectability: For that reason the club could not be called after Mary Wollstonecraft, whose behavior had been unconventional, nor could Eleanor Marx, who lived in an unhappy common-law marriage with Edward Aveling, become a member. Schreiner's desire to write a preface to a republication of Wollstonecraft's *Vindication of the Rights of Woman* (1792), which she would work on sporadically in 1888 after leaving London, probably arose from her usual strong identification with unconventional, socially stigmatized thinkers. She saw it as a chance to "hold the substance of all my thoughts on the man and woman question" (Rive, *Letters,* 136), a project first conceived as a collaborative work with Pearson on the history of women.

Pearson and the intimacy that developed between them thus held out a dream Schreiner had long nurtured: that a working comradeship on an equal basis was possible between men and women. She was undone both by her own desires as a woman, the sexual passion that was being debated politely at the club, her emotional need and vulnerability, and by Pearson's final coldness and rejection of her. He himself seemed to have toyed with the idea of experiments in passion, and Schreiner's letters to him reveal a growing intimacy of tone as well as his private visits to her in London, but, as Walkowitz points out, his attitudes toward women were ambivalent, mixing contempt and desire. Also, his chief female friend, Elizabeth Cobb, who acted as guardian of the club and of Pearson (Ellis thought that they in fact had a love affair, a theory possibly supported by the fact that Cobb suddenly had another baby in her forties after a crisis in her marriage in 1887), regarded Schreiner with a mixture of fascination and envy as a kind of sexual adventuress. Elizabeth Cobb and other women in the club were intrigued and frightened by the new areas of sexual possibility that were opening up, and many emotions swirled around Karl Pearson, culminating in a destructive triangle between Schreiner, Cobb, and Pearson, and a fourth figure— Bryan Donkin, Schreiner's doctor and unwanted but constant suitor. There were dramatic scenes and jealous confrontations, and Schreiner fled from London to the Riviera in December 1886. There had been invasive visits from Elizabeth Cobb, who became a persecutory figure in Schreiner's imagination, and who perhaps in reality played an interfering role. Everybody blamed everybody else for Schreiner's breakdown at the end of 1886, and she left to find her own peace in Alassio and Menton and to repair bridges in the writing of the allegories, the attempt at a preface on Wollstonecraft, and the writing of a new prelude to her incomplete, redrafted version of *From Man to Man*. She had discovered again that complex intimate relationships had a destructive effect on her, but Pearson's rejection was also ice to a wound, as she described it, and she once again found herself free and solitary and able to write. Once more, it was pain that moved her on: "[T]here is nothing helps one like traveling when one is in pain" (Rive, *Letters*, 127). Pearson, she said, had "woke[n] up my ambition, that is, my wish to express myself to others" (Rive, *Letters*, 148). This ambition triggered her writing again and got her through a time of personal suffering and isolation during which she wrote very affectionate letters to Havelock Ellis and Edward Carpenter, turning also, once again, to more impersonal issues such as the first stirrings of labor strikes and the labor movement in England at the time of her departure.

If the Socialist movement could be seen "much more clearly and as a whole" (Rive, *Letters*, 126) after Schreiner left London for Alassio, in Italy, where she found peace and creativity in a landscape similar to the Cape Province of her childhood and girlhood, so could the larger social questions of marriage and autonomy for women. Schreiner reaffirmed her belief in the ideal of "the perfect mental and physical life-long union of one man with one woman" but also her belief that "[o]ur first duty is to develop ourselves" and to be "materially independent" of men (Rive, *Letters*, 145). These insights are pictured in her allegory on the position of women, "Three Dreams in a Desert," which she later said should be read in conjunction with her other polemical work on the position of women, *Woman and Labour*, because it epitomized that work.

Schreiner's first few years in London were thus a crucible for the development of further thoughts and insights about women's lives and divided responsibilities and desires, the difficulties of contemporary relationships for intelligent and idealistic women, and the penalties paid by men at a time when women were struggling for greater independence and were no longer content with the old roles and customs. All of this had been driven home by her experiences within the Men and Women's Club and with Ellis, Pearson, and Cobb; much of it had been argued out in an exchange of letters with Pearson. She realized that she could not behave with free camaraderie among men, "my sex must always divide" (Rive, *Letters*, 126). This drove her into a deeper solidarity with women and a stronger determination that her writing would illuminate the lives of women for women. A recognition of needs and losses brought a sense of what the compensations were: "[B]eing a woman I can reach other women where no man could reach them. A growing tenderness is in my heart for them. I shall never be a man and a brother among you men that I love so, but I have my work" (Rive, *Letters*, 146). The allegories in *Dreams* play out a drama of shifting affiliations with womanhood and brotherhood, with love and androgyny, which embodied the insights of this decade, during which an overwhelming and natural desire for love and children was thwarted and then rechanneled into a deep humanitarian impulse toward humanity and art and their close relationship.

There were two other social catalysts for Schreiner's rethinking of the position of women apart from the Men and Women's Club, although both affected the membership and activities of the club. The first was the disclosure— called "The Maiden Tribute of Modern Babylon"[2]— made by crusading journalist W. T. Stead in *The Pall Mall Gazette* of 1885 that young virgins were being sold into prostitution in London. The topic of child prostitution thus became available for public discussion; Cobb could easily recruit more members for their club and Schreiner, comparing her own response to Ellis's lack of enthusiasm, "wrote and collected women" in protest (Rive, *Letters*, 134). At the same time this "classic Victorian sexual script, based on male dominance and female passivity, the association of sex and violence, and the crossing of class lines in the male pursuit of the female object of desire" (Walkowitz, 42) must have stirred up complex responses in Schreiner, Cobb, and the other women of the club, campaigning as they were for greater female liberty while such evidence of male exploitation and secret violence was being offered in the press. As Walkowitz points out, the women of the club brought to the discussions "a pervasive sense of sexual vulnerability, organized around a specific melodramatic script of sexual danger" (p. 45). It was much easier for the men involved to maintain a distant and scientific tone in discussion; for women whose "own identity was organized around the figure of the prostitute" (Walkowitz, 51), which would include all Victorian women, it was impossible to be abstract and disinterested. These revelations and the intensity of unconscious fears they must have triggered might well have played some role in Schreiner's own collapse at the end of 1886. Of the three women who had had overlapping intimacies with Pearson, Elizabeth Cobb retreated into her marriage and another late pregnancy, Olive Schreiner collapsed and fled to the continent to renew her writing career, and Maria Sharpe, Cobb's younger sister and secretary of the club, became engaged to Pearson, broke down and canceled her engagement, and then married him in 1890, the year before Schreiner published her volume, *Dreams*. While she was writing on the continent, metaphors of childbirth once again replaced any hoped for real marriage and children.

The other social catalyst was the struggle around the repeal of the Contagious Diseases Acts, which were introduced in 1864 to allow medical and police examination of prostitutes in garrison towns and ports. Middle-class reformers and feminists succeeded in repealing the acts in 1886. There was a distinct difference between male and female discourse around the repeal movement: the discourse of sexual hygiene and controlled reproduction that Pearson and other men favored, and the discourse of the medical rape of women, the double standard of sexual behavior, and the female heroism of Josephine Butler, who campaigned for her "fallen sisters." Schreiner's allegory, "I Thought I Stood," draws on this second heroic discourse of sisterhood between middle-class women and prostitutes as the basis of feminism, not the arraignment of men nor the exploitation of prostitutes by "respectable women" who "pick their way" over the bodies of disgraced women: "She was upon the ground in the street, and they passed over her; I lay down by her, and she put her arms around my neck, and so I lifted her, and we two rose together."[3] Here the two usually polarized Victorian female roles are integrated, and "Man" is drawn into the circle of healing; Schreiner's objections to Pearson's paper on the "Woman Question" were that he had left out the other side of the question, Man. Her allegory "Three Dreams in a Desert" reveals her view that men and women are both constrained by false gender roles and expectations although women have suffered more at particular historical junctures from those constraints.

The allegories collected in *Dreams* thus arose from lifelong concerns and artistic affiliations that were reactivated by a confluence of events around Karl Pearson and the Men and Women's Club. *Dreams*—and the artistic sifting and arranging process that took place between 1887 and 1889—represented the shaping of life impulses toward self and others, self and world, which had become agonizingly disorganized in London. At Alassio and Menton, the pain of lost love and solitude persisted, but there was also time for serenity and reflection, time once more to restore balance between her allegiance to herself and her fellow men (Rive, *Let-*

ters, 131). Reflection is an allegorical figure who "steals light out of the past to shed it on the future" (*Dreams,* 19). Allegory offered Schreiner a generic space within which she could meditate on the recent painful flux of life; in that metaphorical haven she could bind up wounds and present didactically to others the conclusions she was reaching about the problematic relationship between autonomy and desire, the artist's need for freedom, and the woman's desire for fulfillment in love.

Dreams: The Politics of Yearning

Feeling bound to speak now on all sides of "the sex question," "woman's intellectual equality (or as I hold, inequality with man), marriage, prostitution" (Rive, *Letters,* 136), the most appropriate and condensed form was achieved by "throwing a thing into the form of an allegory . . . with no loss, but a great gain to clearness" (Rive, *Letters,* 136). Allegory presented itself as her own female response or counterdiscourse to "the rationalist discourse on sex . . . that silenced women, and that denied and suppressed some of the terrible secrets about sexual danger and its misogynist origins that women felt" (Walkowitz, 56). Schreiner argues that her allegories tell a more complete truth than rationalist discourse by presenting a more complete, lived reality in poetically ordered narrative: "As soon as there is the form and the spirit, the passion and the thought, then there is poetry, or the living reality" (Rive, *Letters,* 142). At the same time she wanted to retain some of the polemical strengths of prose and not sink into an easy, lulling prose poetry that was tempting because "there's such a delicious sensation going through all your body as if the whole of it was keeping time" (Rive, *Letters,* 155). This points to a sensual, erotic element in the allegories, although they are often about the renunciation of desire. The rhythm of the allegories can reenact yearning in language that replaces the lost lover while affirming feminist truths in the realm of the symbolic.

Schreiner arranged her "dreams" chronologically so that the collection recharts her past experience up until the time of her departure from England. The first allegory, "The Lost Joy," dated back to the Gau relationship: the first experience of lost love and the writing that took its place. The allegorized figures are a couple who pass from early joy to a more perfect phase of love and sympathy. Since Schreiner finished it in London, the implication is that she had learned, especially in her relationship with Ellis, that love could take different forms. This insight is further developed in the last and longest allegory in the collection, "The

Sunlight Lay Across My Bed," in which there are three heavens: "In the least Heaven sex reigns supreme; in the higher it is not noticed; but in the highest it does not exist" (*Dreams*, 175). Although the vision is of an inhuman transcendence, it is created in order to redeem and transfigure the everyday London world, where a "broken barrel-organ" plays and a "a long yellow streak of pale London sunlight" plays across the dreamer's bed as she/he awakes in the real world. This allegory presented Schreiner's vision of the spirit of socialism, a love and brotherhood that would change the living hell of exploited labor and capitalism, imaged in the picture of hell and its winepresses in the first section of the allegory.

The second allegory is that of the hunter, excerpted from *African Farm;* the arrangement of the volume reveals that the three longest allegories relate to one another. "The Hunter" is the late Victorian philosophical allegory of social evolution and present renunciation; it presents the role of the pathbreaker for the modern world: the man who seeks truth in a new spirit of impassioned inquiry that disdains old dogmas and worn-out creeds and endures loneliness and ostracism as a result. It is an allegory on time and mortality. Love and work are key concerns— and the only realities. Rewards are few, and much must be renounced; the hunter must set free even his last beautiful bird, called Immortality. This hidden bird or flower, the last to be renounced, is a motif that recurs in different contexts. It evokes different possibilities: the desire to be loved, to be remembered after death, to leave a child as a stake in the future, to be famous, or to experience human companionship. The lesson of stern renunciation is a Puritan one, yet it lends itself to a social critique of worn-out convention and stultifying religious dogma.

In "Three Dreams in a Desert," which is a feminist version of the Hunter allegory, the setting is much more realistic and African, and the dreamer is a generic Schreiner figure, out in a semidesert terrain dotted with mimosas, falling into a sequence of dreams about the struggle for liberty by Woman, a creature buried in sand and at first unable to move. As Monsman points out, these figures are "heroically idealized" and enact "the monumental drama of the race and gender" (1992, 56). The first dream in the desert elucidates women's long phase of subjugation when men dominated in the "Age of Muscular Force." The "Age of Nervous Force and Mechanical Invention"—the Industrial Revolution— found women weakened by their historical inactivity and unable to rise, except by their own efforts. The second dream, set on the banks of an African river, shows the next phase, during which women find the way to new activity by throwing off dependence and convention and laying down "the hidden child": passion (although also the children that could flow from passion). The path to freedom is solitary and goes through labor and suffering, but the early generations are like locusts whose bodies compose a bridge for future generations, for "the entire human race." These are feminist tropes of heroic endeavor, solitary sacrifice, and labor to bring about a different future. The third brief dream portrays that future, in which men and women are equal comrades, when friendship and love have created a heaven on earth. This allegory had a great influence on contemporary women and those involved in the struggle for women's suffrage, greater personal liberty, and professional training, and it makes moving reading in its clear relationship to the lived experience of women like Schreiner.

Set at Santa Croce in Alassio, a favorite place for meditation and retreat, "In a Ruined Chapel" comes closest to the Pearson drama but generalizes that experience to narrate the process that creates forgiveness, a process in which a basic fellow humanity is recognized and restored. Here the olive trees, the pacifist symbol associated with her name and with both the Mediterranean and the Cape Province, are mentioned in association with the ice plant (*Mesembryanthemum crystallinum L.*), the succulent Karoo plant that is a recurrent motif for microcosmic beauty, stored strength, and the pattern behind creation in *African Farm.*

The sequence of allegories is quite complex and telling, moving from a more traditional drama around human love, in which female passivity is set against possible agency ("she was waiting—she was waiting; but she could not tell for what," p. 13) to the more active dreamer, shifting from male to female, who calls up vision more strenuously to combat and redeem social ills and distorting or exploitative social structures. The dreamer gives way to a framed figure who is roused into difficult activity and by whom the dreamer in the frame is refreshed and reenergized and enabled to return to daily realities with new hope and vigor.

Dreams became a hugely popular volume and was translated into many languages. It spoke to the turn-of-the-century fondness for prose poetry and experiments with different media and art forms; it appealed to a growing audience of women who looked for their own aspirations in print. Its cri de coeur, "Freedom before Love," was a heroic battle cry for the first generation of women struggling to break away from traditional social constraints on public training and personal fulfillment. Although it encoded and released Schreiner from a set of private disappointments, her experience was also representative, and she was not frightened of serving as an example in the hope that her pain, dramatized and allegorized, would be of use to others. At Alassio and Menton, she came to understand the historical dimensions of her struggle during the London years.

Allegory and Postcolonial Critique

Schreiner's fiction is now increasingly viewed in terms of allegory, and allegory itself has gained a central place as a genre that enables postcolonial vision. The novels have been understood in terms of allegory, as setting "artifice in realistic frames" (Gorak, 53) and portraying the self as "a set of imperfect cultural mirrors." Wilson Harris speaks of the centrality of allegorical vision as a "double vision" that allows the "doubled loyalties" of the colonial writer some play (Gorak, 68).[4] Allegory is seen as destabilizing the linear narrative of colonial and male authority. As Irene Gorak has argued of Schreiner's writing, "allegory is her recurring trope and colonial life her recurring topic." She points out, too, that the figural center of Schreiner's allegory is the human, female body (p. 67). Able to mutate into the body of the woman artist—the solitary pathfinder whose blood is the artist's medium—this body often links up with other female bodies. It does so, for example, in the image of locusts crossing the stream, an adapted evolutionary image that suggests the impersonality of a historical body, the mass of women imprisoned in history but struggling through its material reality. The shifting sexual identity of the dreamer or quester conveys the ways in which women were compelled to adopt a male persona in order to become heroic and active in the world, although effects of historical pathos are gained when the quester is envisioned as specifically female, as in "Three Dreams in a Desert," and having to renounce specifically female methods of fulfillment, such as giving birth to children.

But the chief achievement of the allegories may lie in Schreiner's readiness to cast her pacifist, reformist vision of sexual and social relations into limpid parables that were faithful to the pain of her own personal lessons in South Africa and London. These lessons were that it was quite difficult for a woman like herself to survive independently as a professional writer and a single woman and that, whether in Africa or London, the social norms for women's lives were profoundly destructive of free work, love, and companionship. This had implications for colonial relations: "As the colony stands to the metropolis and the allegory to the encoded truth, so the female stands to the male. Women are pictures to men, who respond generously to their beauty and creativity while ignorantly provoking their self-inflicted pain" (Gorak, 67).

Schreiner's greater understanding of the social restrictions of gender norms came to her through bitter experiences, and by casting them in the concrete, compact form of brief allegories, she kept open a valuable gap between experience and story into which each woman could read her own meanings and insert her own story of womanhood. This is why the prelude to *From Man to Man*, written in early 1889, was such an achievement in its bridging of autobiography and allegory. It has been characterized by feminist critics as creating "an elsewhere of vision"[5] by being both an invented allegory of the main character's adult life as well as a re-creation of scenes from Schreiner's own childhood. Laura Donaldson sees the prelude as both allegory and metanarrative, a story about the ways in which women weave stories, thus negotiating "the contradiction between a radical politics of identity and a postmodernist skepticism" (Donaldson, 132). The allegory that so powerfully arose in her unconscious mind in 1889 and was then perceived as an organic preface to the novel about Bertie and Rebekah could be seen as the crowning allegory of the decade for her, the twin sisters of childhood deeply uniting those aspects of herself that had become painful psychic antagonists. It is significant that almost immediately she set about planning her return to South Africa, the prelude constituting a fresh start to the book that would endlessly preoccupy her as the book of her unfinished life.

Schreiner's achievement in the allegories and in the writings of which the allegories were a part was that they highlighted the power inequalities of a colonial society. Furthermore, they revealed that the same gender and class imbalances existed in London, the heart of darkness from which the settlers and missionaries had first set out to "civilize" Africa. It is then doubly ironic that Schreiner herself, delighted by the prospect of her approaching return to Africa—at the time of the Great Dock Strike of 1889 that lit up East End faces "with a large idea" (Rive, *Letters*, 156)—should have become preoccupied with what she called the "savage." "I'm reading about nothing but savages," she told Edward Carpenter, while thanking him for his gift of socialist sandals. And on board the *Norham Castle* in Dartmouth, just before sailing on 11 October 1889: "Goodbye, dear old Brother. You will have to come out after me some day, when you hear about the stars and the black people and all the nice things. I'm going to be quite well. Goodbye" (Rive, *Letters*, 157).

A major chapter of her life had closed, and she had learned to adapt a metropolitan form and fin de siècle Symbolist mode to tell and to disguise her personal truths as a colonial woman. She would live in South Africa again from 1890 to 1913, during an era of intense British imperialism that would precipitate war and lead to the formation of the white-controlled Union of South Africa in 1910. During this period, when the foundations of a modern, racist, capitalist state were being laid, her non-fictional, polemical interventions in political life would take precedence over other forms of writing.

Chapter Six

Parables and Pamphlets: Olive Schreiner in South Africa, 1891–1913

During the years that Schreiner was in Europe, the scramble for Africa had begun in earnest at the Berlin Conference of 1884. The penetration of the "Dark Continent" by European explorers had become the most exciting narrative of the late nineteenth century. While Schreiner was compiling her *Dreams,* the rather rhapsodic, agonistic result of an actual South African woman's sojourn and suffering in a metropolis, other authors were capitalizing on the sense of adventure and British national prestige brought about by African explorers like James Grant, Samuel White Baker, David Livingstone, and Henry Stanley. Stanley's *In Darkest Africa* was an 1890 bestseller in England, selling 150,000 copies.[1] Thus the discourses that legitimated the British Empire and consolidated England's sense of moral superiority after the abolition of slavery in England were being widely circulated as Schreiner reentered the maelstrom of South African political life in the 1890s. During this crucial decade, Cecil Rhodes, as Prime Minister of the Cape Colony and Kimberley mining magnate, attempted to annex and orchestrate a British-controlled South Africa and to move his financial empire northward from the Cape Colony. "I would annex the planets if I could" was one of his more quotable and unabashed maxims. Rhodes would be the instrument of the British Empire in South Africa during the nineties and also a cause of its downfall.

Patrick Brantlinger has argued that "the myth of the Dark Continent developed during the transition from the main British campaign against the slave trade, which culminated in the outlawing of slavery in all British territory in 1833, to the partitioning of Africa which dominated the final quarter of the nineteenth century" (p. 185). He suggests that the antislavery campaign and imperialism form a continuum rather than a contradiction; "abolitionism contained the seeds of Empire" (p. 186) because both were products of British economic interests. During the

1890s, South Africa witnessed an increasing tension between the supposed "civilizing" mission in Africa and the economic annexation it masked. In 1895 the Jameson Raid—an aborted coup against the Transvaal—occurred at Chamberlain's and Rhodes's bidding. The Anglo-Boer War (1899–1902) sowed bitter seeds between English-speakers and Boers and laid the groundwork for the treatment of the indigenous population when the Afrikaner later came into political power.

The British declared themselves saviors of the African while at the same time licensing Cecil Rhodes to bribe his way into Cape politics. At the same time, the British South Africa Company, empowered by a Royal Charter, engaged in kraal-burning, looting, and rape while putting down the Matabele "uprisings" in Matabeleland and Mashonaland, then called southern Zambesia. Schreiner's achievement in *Trooper Peter Halket of Mashonaland* (1897) was to put before the public, especially the British public (her target audience), the atrocities practiced daily in the region and to show the moral tensions and divisions within a supposedly Christian and civilized colonizing force.[2] South Africa became the crucible of Schreiner's developing understanding of the relationship between a patriarchal society and British imperialism. She perceived that the double moral standards affected all women and black South Africans to different degrees and that neither group had "the same powers and right[s]" as white men partly because neither was "his equal in the eye of the law."[3] They could therefore be treated as dependents, exchanged as property, dehumanized, sexually violated, and even killed in the name of a "war" that bore a curious likeness to economic advance, class mobility for working-class Englishmen like Halket, and patronage of the "noble savage." Schreiner's key perception of the decade was of the particular ways in which the emancipatory struggles of women and subject races were analogous; her principal works from 1891 to 1913—*Trooper Peter Halket* (1897) and *Woman and Labour* (1911)—demonstrate an uneven, complex but constant allegiance to the ways in which racism and sexism were inexorably intertwined. In *Thoughts on South Africa*, Schreiner argues explicitly that "the disabilities attaching to sex or class, which in our most civilized societies still exist" are the "lineal descendants of slavery" (p. 105).

Schreiner's thinking during these two decades was inevitably bound up with the experiences of her personal life, which were inseparable from the political struggles in which she, her husband S. C. Cronwright, and important members of her family were vehemently embroiled. She and her siblings were often on opposite sides of issues such as the Anglo-Boer War and other political conflicts between the British colonies, the Cape and Natal, and the two republics in the north, the Transvaal and the Orange Free State. In *Trooper Peter Halket*, a conflict between a preacher of conscience and his wife symbolizes the emotional rifts that were opened up in South African families as the English troops looted and pillaged in the north, killed Boers, burned farms, and put Boer women into concentration camps. Resolutely loyal to traditional "British" ideals of justice, truth, and law, to the country once perceived as home, and to the indigenous people—Boer and Black—among whom they had grown up, women like Schreiner were grievously tested and became South Africans of a new order in the process. On the eve of the Anglo-Boer War, the drama of deeply divided allegiances felt by many English-speaking South Africans were articulated in the vibrant appeal she launched: *An English-South African's View of the Situation* (1899).[4] Here she pointed out that South Africa's only wealth—its gold and diamonds—was not only being removed into foreign hands, mainly British, but was also funding English military aggression against South Africa. Her assessment was right on target. As the Transvaal became a power in its own right and threatened to bring about an independent "United States of South Africa," anxiety increased in England over the possible loss of the Cape Colony as the key to the Eastern trade route and to England's naval defense.[5] The British government was in thrall to Rhodes's wealth and his ability to manipulate the Afrikaner Bond in the Cape to support his expansionist aims in Africa. According to some historians, the war was generated by a sense of the waning of British Empire and "new and extremist notions of the empire's importance for Britain's future greatness" (Robinson et al., 460). South Africa was regarded as "strategically vital and politically unreliable" (Robinson et al., 461). Schreiner was correct about the alliance between Rhodes's mineral wealth and the determination to maintain British dominance by war, if necessary. The British Empire would go to war in 1899 "for a cause that was lost, for a grand illusion" (Robinson et al., 461). In her pamphlet she recognized that the bloodshed soon to ensue would para-doxically deepen South African loyalties and bind English South Africans to Boers: "You will not kill us with your Lee-Metfords; you will make us" (*ESAV*, 90).

Schreiner's older siblings, Theo and Ettie, her niece, Katie Stuart, and her indefatigable mother, Rebecca Lyndall, admired and supported Rhodes and his dream of a South Africa united under the British flag, while Olive and her husband Cron were progressively drawn into becoming Rhodes's chief opponents, exposing bribery and corruption under his administration as well as his treatment of the "Native." They saw Rhodes and his backers in England ruthlessly exploiting the land, mineral wealth, and the Native population. Theo and Ettie, on the other hand, exhibited a more simplistic missionary fervor and were more pro-British; they perceived the British as their mother did, as saving the indigenous inhabitants from the exploitation of the Boers. In England this view was shared by philanthropic societies such as the Aborigines Protection Society. Rhodes's activities in Matabeleland and Mashonaland brought these personal and political tensions to a head, as in that terrain, freer of the rule of law, the brutal practices that enabled annexation of the land were more clearly visible. In exposing the campaign in Matabeleland and Mashonaland, Schreiner disclosed the nexus of imperial interests working with loyalist colonials in South Africa as a whole to disenfranchise the African people.

Schreiner's responses to Rhodes were at first ambivalent, a mixture of attraction to the grandeur of his schemes, which had been presented to her as humanitarian, and mistrust. She also admired the male explorer who traveled freely into the hinterland, which for a moment she saw herself as doing when she returned to Africa to visit for the first time a terrain perceived since childhood as magical and powerful:

> From there we believed the Queen of Sheba brought the peacocks and the gold for King Solomon . . . Yes, we should go and see it. Up a valley, a great white rhinoceros would wade with its feet in the water; on each side under the trees zebra and antelopes would stand quietly feeding on the green grass. . . . The very names Zambezi and Limpopo drew us, with the lure of the unknown. (*TSA*, 46–47)

Schreiner later demythologizes this terrain in the name of contemporary history in *Trooper Peter Halket of Mashonaland*. In her essays written during the nineties, she presented the history and geography and inhabitants of South Africa to a British audience, seeing herself as a bridging cultural figure and commentator (a role that the British and the American press partly reinforced). She projected Mashonaland as a possible nature preserve for South African flora and fauna. Clearly, then, Rhodes's aims in the territory were completely opposed to Schreiner's pacifist, conservationist vision, and yet at first she had found him attractive and had flirted with him. An admirer of *The Story of an African Farm*, he had just become Prime Minister of the Cape at the time she was a returning celebrity. When shortly thereafter she discovered the nature and scope of his ambitions and the crassness with which he expressed them, he became not only the target of her satire but also the man she felt she needed to save from "a downward course" (Rive, *Letters*, 268). An astute political observer, she saw the nature of his campaign to win votes and power, and from the time he openly supported the Strop Bill in Parliament, which licensed the flogging of farm servants, she withdrew her interest. She became allied with, and later married in February of 1894, the man who publicly denounced Rhodes, Samuel Cron Cronwright, whose direct masculinity she was attracted to while perceiving that he shared certain qualities with Rhodes, including arrogance and obstinacy. The Cronwright-Schreiners (her husband's readiness to take her name indicates his sympathy with her feminist standpoint) became united in their opposition to Rhodes, to the British invasion of the Republics during the war, and to the alliance of capitalism and imperialism that Rhodes represented. These struggles would strengthen the Cronwright-Schreiners' sympathies with the indigenous inhabitants despite the patronizing tone and the evolutionary rhetoric they sometimes unthinkingly espoused as a natural outgrowth of their background and socialization. Their empathy with the Boers also deepened; as Karel Schoeman points out, this compassion is markedly present, although partially and sometimes emotively portrayed, in the essays of the nineties later collected as *Thoughts on South Africa*. Nobody would find their loyalties clear-cut during this decade of conflict between British, Boer, and Black, in which the black majority would be the sacrifices and the losers for a century to come.

At this time the agents of historical change were still seen as the "civilized" whites, with blacks as the objects of either violent appropriation or charitable impulses. The Hottentots, in keeping with the evolutionary hierarchy of the chain of being, were always perceived as "the eternal children of the human race" (*TSA*, 96). In Schreiner's own vision, despite her empathy with slave figures from her earliest short story, indigenous people were seen as part of the landscape, one in which servants were taken for granted. She and her husband of five years left Johannesburg at the outbreak of war, a time when she had had the last of a series of miscarriages and had been seriously ill. The flavor of her relationship at this time with the Karoo landscape and its people is conveyed in the following description: "There are 23 dogs here and 500 ostriches, and there are sheep and horses, and coloured and black servants, and lovely koppjes on which the sun shines at sunset, as it only can in the Karoo, it is all so beautiful and restful . . . It seems like heaven" (Schoeman 1992, 12). The indigenous people are seen as an organic, creaturely part of a mute landscape in which farm animals and domestic labor are natural constituents. The connections between the indentured laborers from whom her first protagonist, the colored slave/apprentice, Jannita, is drawn and these "black and coloured servants" on a restful Karoo farm are not made. Yet it was precisely her own sufferings as a woman, one who progressively discovered the inequities and double standards built into marriage and society, that enabled her to identify more and more strongly with the rights of an oppressed black population and to present vividly and passionately, as in *Trooper Peter Halket*, an analysis of colonial patriarchy and the need for the practice of Christian compassion and justice. She was extremely proud of having written *Trooper Peter*, partly because it cost her a great deal in terms of family relationships, but also because she felt she had honored the truths told to her by people who had witnessed events such as the lynching depicted in the notorious frontispiece to the volume, in which white men stand around nonchalantly while three dead black figures dangle from a "hanging tree" in Matabeleland. The photograph was censored after the first edition and not restored until a later edition. It points to the Christian typology inscribed in the story and to the historical atrocities perpetrated during the campaign of the British South Africa Company, the "Chartered Company" (it secured a royal charter in July 1889) that was establishing "Rhodesia."

The "Chartered Company," of which Trooper Peter is a hapless, naive member, demonstrating company ideology from the ground up, "cast the mantle of empire over a gigantic speculation in mineral futures" (Robinson, 250). Peter's financial hopes around company flotation and gold shares reflect this alliance. The company was an instrument "to divert South Africa's commercial development towards political unity and an imperial dominion" and also "an admission that the British government was losing its power to shape South Africa's destiny directly" (Robinson, 251).

Thoughts on South Africa

In one of her allegories, Schreiner represents the supreme gift to the artist such as herself as idealistic vision: "[T]he ideal shall be real to thee" (*Dreams*, 96). At the same time, *Thoughts on South Africa* and, more particularly, her letters during these years, reveal that she grasped the political repercussions of the events of the nineties better than many others who were political leaders. She overestimated the power of any purely literary or personal intervention in the events leading up to war, yet the influence of literary interventions such as *Trooper Peter* is undeniable and grows in retrospect as the events she predicted—the swampy, lingeringly destructive outcome of a refusal to treat black South Africans as human equals with equal rights—have come to pass and will take ages to undo. In a sense, therefore, she was realistic in depicting events in the political world while at the same time remaining faithful to the ideals she saw as guaranteed by English civilization at its best, that same civilization in whose name the "inchoate trading firm" of a greedy empire operated, "seeking to dominate by force peoples and lands all over the world" (*TSA*, 50). This aspect of her vision is evident in her description of the Karoo landscape and perspective while living in Hanover during the war:

> If I go outside on to the flat I can see distinctly as far as there is anything to see. Fifty miles away, as the crow flies, is Spitz Kop (Compass Berg), 8,000 feet high, jutting into the blue sky as though its edges were cut with a diamond. I can, even with the naked eye, see the krantz on it. Things do not fade away or become absorbed in a haze here; they grow small in the distance, but they remain clear. (Schoeman 1992, 119)

This long-distance view of the immeasurable harm done by the Chartered Company, the Jameson Raid, and the Anglo-Boer War is a characteristic of her writings at this time. This clear-cut image could well be used as the story of Peter Halket's conversion and death draws to a close. The figures of the mounted troopers recede into the distance, with a Colonial and an Englishman riding "on after the troop" (*TPH*, 122) in Mashonaland, perhaps unchanged by Peter's death but certainly affected by it. The complex effect of individual actions and the way in which they make history is one of Schreiner's constant themes. History exists within individual consciousness, which is where she most often locates conflict.

In *Thoughts on South Africa* Schreiner posits the challenge she saw facing South Africa at the time: "How, from our political states and discordant races, can a great, a healthy, a united, an organized nation be formed?" (p. 57). She founds the hope for this inevitable nationhood on the indissoluble bond between South Africans that is subtle but real, "our mixture of races itself." Empires and nations cannot be founded on "racial hatred and force" (p. 58). Her predictions here are worth quoting fully: "[I]f the South Africa of the future is to remain eaten internally by race hatreds, a film of culture and intelligence spread over seething masses of ignorance and brutality, intersupport and union being wholly lacking; then . . . our doom is sealed; our place will be wanting among the great, free nations of the earth" (p. 58). She argues here that South Africa faced a unique problem in that "Our race question is complicated by a question of colour, which presents itself to us in a form more virulent and intense than that in which it has met many modern people. America and India have nothing analogous to it; and it has to be faced in an age which does not allow of the old methods in dealing with alien and so-called inferior peoples. In South Africa the nineteenth century is brought face to face with a prehistoric world" (59). This quotation neatly illustrates that the concept of race had a broader basis than color and that the Boer and the Englishman, as she describes them, were representatives of broad racial categories, the former indigenous and unique, the latter imported but distinct from the "home" variety. The "Englishman" is so much a conceptual category within racial morphology that "he" is also gender neutral and can take different, gendered forms: She writes that "he" can be a "little liquor-seller" with "a wagon full of bad brandy made by the Boers," or "a female missionary, buried in a remote native village to instruct heathen girls and women," or a "cultured, sympathetic, freedom-loving man," or one "tying up and flogging to death his black brothers" (p. 278).

Although these enormous moral variations exist within the racial category, the Englishman who has become the Colonial in Africa is also distinguished from the Boer by his language, which ties him to "the birthplace of his speech" (p. 73). However, the "Taal," the Afrikaans language that developed from Dutch—and whose staying power Schreiner underestimated—was indigenous. This underlies Schreiner's sense of always being part of her "motherland," which had produced numerous masterpieces in the English language. It supports her sense of belonging to a great stream of English eloquence dating back to the *Bible* and Bunyan, and it bolsters the satire she aims, in *Peter Halket*, at the colonial slang, whose crudities inscribe and legitimate the rapacity of British imperialism. She also suggests that a definition of the Boer can be derived more accurately from language usage and cultural isolation than from race. Boer means "a South African by descent whose vernacular is the Taal, and who uses familiarly no literary European language" (p. 91). Landscape in South Africa is thus imbued with a linguistic dimension; discourse inscribes power relations and evacuates the reality of those who are "othered," silenced and dehumanized by a desire for domination and control.[6] *Trooper Peter* is partly a display of the processes by which imperialism legitimates itself in a foreign terrain by making evident the innermost consciousness of "colonial man."

Trooper Peter Halket of Mashonaland

As Stephen Gray has argued,[7] *Trooper Peter* is a study in "colonial man" that reveals him to be a "mama's boy" who distinguishes between white womanhood as an icon of protective maternity and black women as unfeeling chattels who can be raped or bartered for brandy because they are not English and not white: "Then he thought suddenly of a black woman he and another man caught alone in the bush, her baby on her back, but young and pretty. Well, they didn't shoot her!—and a black woman wasn't white! His mother didn't understand these things; it was all so different in England from South Africa" (pp. 36–37). This is an early literary demonstration of how imperial discourse constructs the native terrain as completely different, thus rationalizing behavior that is clearly outside the law. It sets up black women as the legitimate prey of the sons of Englishwomen in Africa simply because they are obviously distinct from English women. The passage goes on to indicate the stirrings of conscience in Peter during his nighttime vigil on a koppie while separated from his troop, stirrings that will lead to his later conversion to "Christ's company" and a successful attempt to free a black man (the husband of a woman he has earlier stolen away and impregnated) from imprisonment and death.

Trooper Peter Halket deviates from all of Schreiner's earlier fictions in that the focus shifts from the struggles of sympathetic young colonial children and young women to the consciousness of a male colonizer previously presented mainly from without. She had presented Bonaparte Blenkins farcically and externally in *African Farm*, and she briefly enters the consciousness of a conventional colonial English husband, Frank, in *From Man to Man*. Working-class in origin and lured toward South Africa by dreams of opportunity and the wealth that he will share with his washerwoman mother, the young male protagonist in *Trooper Peter* is shown to have acclimatized himself to brutal colonial behavior and discourse, although his conscience troubles him when he has time for reflection. This he does on the long night that makes up the temporal

setting of the major part of the narrative (pp. 1–94). During this night
Jesus Christ appears to him as the voice of Peter's own conscience as he
falls asleep after brooding on the burning of the native kraals and the
dynamiting of a cave. In "the burning core" of a log breaking open on
the nighttime fire, he sees vivid images of people dying under machine
guns, "the skull of an old Mashona blown off at the top" (p. 36), and the
young woman he has raped. Christ is treated as a literal personage as
well as an animation of the suffering martyr for humanity, with eyes
that recall to Peter the eyes of his mother. Their dialogue is presented
with satirical humor and liveliness, with Christ's silences and anger
looming as a backdrop to Peter's rationalizing chatter about his exploits
in Mashonaland. While Schreiner was on vacation at the Kowie River,
this "allegory story" suddenly occurred to her as a symbolic summation
of the historical crux of the decade. What is unusual about the tale is
that the dreamer or visionary is untypically the male colonizer—not the
woman visionary. This draws Peter within the sympathies of a human
family even as it reveals the cultural mechanisms that make them dan-
gerous and destructive: social mobility, hero worship, colonial lore, and a
rationalization of native behavior that paints them as rebels and inhuman, immoral others. Peter is a bit of a woman, like Gregory Rose,
which partly redeems the masculinity that is defined within imperial
paradigms and given sexual license on the frontiers of a colony. This
linking of weakness and effeminacy with conventional patriarchal discourse about "woman's place" interests Schreiner as a revelation that
even the weakest link within a patriarchal chain enjoys its benefits.

One of the key images of the narrative is of a cave, a place of shelter
for wounded men and women, of self-sacrifice and death, and for with-
drawal from the war raging all around. The cave has been dynamited by
Peter and his troop, although two women "were left unhurt behind a
fallen rock" (p. 61). This image returns us to Schreiner's first story,
"Dream Life and Real Life," in which the slave Jannita hides and sleeps
in a cave after running away from the cruel farm and where she finds the
comfort and consolation of nature. Twice the cave in *Peter Halket* is made
a place of self-sacrifice by Christ's narrative; in one scene an older
woman shelters a younger until her child is born and then sacrifices her
food rations to her so that she may escape. In another a servant rescues
his kind white prospector employer and is killed in his place, although
the old prospector dies, too. These episodes set the stage for the sacrifice
that ends the novel, but the cave is also interesting as an image of
secrecy and vulnerability, an image of womb and tomb. In 1895 the

Cronwright-Schreiners' only child, a girl, had died shortly after birth, a wound that never quite healed and a loss that played its part in their gradual alienation from each other. In this story, the girl who is raped carries a baby on her back. Yet inside the cave of Christ's story, a young woman gives birth, aided by an old woman, and escapes. At the end of the story the husband of the woman Peter has stolen (both of whom are from Lo Magundis, the seat of native resistance to the Chartered Company) is liberated by Peter, who dies in his place. Thus a man, a young woman, and a newborn child are liberated within the realm of the symbolic; in addition, the historical story of a white colonial family, the Cronwright-Schreiners, is redeemed by the replacement of a black family from within the oppressed people, a family constantly shattered by colonial pillage and war. Schreiner's own deepest woundings are inscribed within this narrative of colonial oppression, and the Oedipal drama of a young white mama's boy is acted out as Peter restores to the black husband his legitimate wife, the mature sexual woman Peter had coveted and stolen.

The focus in this "novel" (the difficulty in classification is a sign of the generic boundaries broken by the narrative) is on black rather than white women, apart from Peter's mother, who symbolizes pure womanhood, the Angel in the House. Completely powerless and hunted like animals, black women are depicted as even more damagingly stereotyped and bartered than the white women of Schreiner's other novels. The woman Peter wants is exchanged for a vat of brandy; this colonial bartering of women extends and vulgarizes the indigenous practice of *lobola* (bridewealth), in which women were goods to be exchanged for cattle. Her capacity for labor is described, but she is not endowed with any "white" moral virtues in Peter's mind. In fact, her double usefulness as concubine and laborer anticipates the future uses of black South African women, tolerated in white areas only if they fulfilled white needs. The narrative as a whole satirizes colonial discourse, and in its symbolism and religious typology enacts a didactic drama of martyrdom, sacrifice, and conversion. Like abolitionist narratives, as Brantlinger has pointed out, it reveals atrocities and uses "the exposé style of abolitionist propaganda" (p. 189). The shocking frontispiece was meant to work in tandem with the exposé style to reveal historical injustices in South Africa.

The second section of the narrative, a brief daytime scene and postlude to the long allegorical dream of part 1, is partly narrated by one of three Colonials, a group offset by a lounging figure of "uncertain nationality," currently "reported to have done three years' labour for attempted rape in Australia" (p. 97). This realistic discourse is dominated by the copresence of rape and colonial annexation of the land. It mediates Peter's conflict with the conventional captain and his own attempt to save the Lo Magundis man, now tied to a tree (one identical to the hanging tree of the frontispiece). The black prisoner has also been hiding in a cave, found "by a little path he tramped down to the water, trodden hard, just like a porcupine's walk" (p. 104). This image is in stark contrast to Schreiner's prelude for the young girl who wanders around in the grass, treading a path before she daydreams a story. Rather, in part 2 of *Trooper Peter,* the image is put to a propagandist, political use. It makes vivid the suffering of blacks that is a part of what Peter now describes as "fighting for freedom," probably the first usage of the term "freedom fighter," which would later become quite familiar in South African liberation struggles. Peter's behavior is framed by the colonial discourse concerning "bush madness" ("bosbevok" in more graphic Afrikaans) as an explanation for compassionate behavior. Bush madness in South Africa is a precursor to becoming a "Kafferboetie" (one who loves the natives too much and thinks they should be treated as equals). It is significant that this concept exists in other dialects of colonial powers: "tropenkollered"in Dutch, recorded by Ian Watt (Brantlinger, 212), or, in more formal English, "maddened by the tropics" or "going native." Conrad's *Heart of Darkness* presents different versions of going native, with that of Kurtz being the most extreme, the emissary of light given over to obscure "savage" rites in the forest. Schreiner writes an earlier version of Kurtz's story (*Heart of Darkness* was serialized in 1899), showing a youthful emissary of British civilization who is impressionable enough to be converted to a different view of the native people by a calm mature presence, that of the Christ visitant, who combines the qualities of an angry father and a merciful mother. Schreiner is careful to include the atrocities against native women, which always take a different, more sexual form than atrocities against men, and to relate those atrocities to a dehumanization made possible by a Victorian overemphasis on pure white womanhood as inseparable from maternity, the "mothers and sisters" for whom one of the Colonials is prepared to "blow people's brains out" (p. 99). Protection of pure mothers and sisters, the colonial moral panic Doris Lessing would later explore in *The Grass is Singing,* is revealed as complementary to the rape of black women. Both involve a violent response to outsiders depending on an internal repression of mature sexuality and on a rigid construction of masculine codes of behavior. Schreiner's satirical allegory in *Trooper Peter* calls attention to the neglected humanity and rights of black women as wives and mothers and reintegrates, in the realm of the symbolic, the shattered black family. Thus *Trooper Peter* can be said to be a narrative written in opposition to adventure yarns that romanticize hidden treasure and women and that make women a sexual symbol for the land itself. Schreiner's fable shows the violation of black women (closely linked with children in the detail of the story) to be central to the colonizing project. It is a founding narrative for later formulations (such as J. M. Coetzee's *Dusklands*)[8] of the marauding colonial exploiters in South Africa. It is also the first attempt to shape contemporary political conflicts over racial issues in South Africa into convincing, naturalistic dialogue, a skill Nadine Gordimer would later greatly expand in her fiction.

Schreiner's own description of *Trooper Peter* as "a sort of allegory story" (Rive, *Letters*, 288) is an accurate one. The narrative draws on many of the features of classical allegory: It is used for "didactic and moral suasion"; as Northrop Frye suggests, there is a typical preponderance of thematic content; it contains elements of irony and religious ritual; and it enacts a "symbolic power struggle" aimed at provoking self-criticism at a time when people were being lulled into inaction by daily routines.[9] As political allegory, its humor purports to disguise the attack and perhaps protect from official retaliation or censorship. The hero's journey enacts an inner movement toward vision and liberation or death after struggle; the hero has strengths as well as weaknesses and is both man and god (caught up in the name of the disciple, Simon Peter). Although there is a "doubleness of intention" typical of allegory (Fletcher, 7), not everyone would grasp the secondary meaning, which lies in the hero's function as a "generator of other secondary personalities, which are aspects of himself" (Fletcher, 35). *Trooper Peter* becomes a richer narrative when Christ and the Lo Magundis black man are seen to be aspects of Peter himself, respectively his higher conscience and his sexual energy and individuality, although they are also more than that and work at other levels of the narrative. The imprisoned black man is also the captured slave of abolitionist narrative: "The black man hung against the white stem, so closely bound to it that they seemed one. His hands were tied to his sides, and his head drooped on his breast. His eyes were closed; and his limbs, which had once been those of a powerful man, had fallen away, making the joints stand out. The wool on his head was wild and thick with neglect, and stood out roughly in long strands;

and his skin was rough with want and exposure. The riems had cut a little into his ankles; and a small flow of blood had made the ground below his feet dark" (p. 117). When the man understands that he has been set free, "Without a word, without a sound, as the tiger leaps when the wild dogs are on it, with one long smooth spring, as though unwounded and unhurt, he turned and disappeared into the grass" (p. 118). This figure symbolizes, as did Jannita in "Dream Life and Real Life," the atrocious conditions of forced labor, punishment, and dehumanization of the indigenous people during the pioneering phase of South African colonialism; it also signifies the day of future reckoning that would herald their emancipation from that order. These conditions of forced labor and domestic slavery on the frontier are only now being more accurately described in revisionary historiography.[10]

The imagery of the narrative prophetically draws on the mingled blood of blacks and whites as the necessary sacrifice that soaks the ground on which a new order may grow. Christ foretells that "the day shall come" when, in that same land where "today the cries of the wounded and the curses of revenge ring in the air," men will "stand shoulder to shoulder, white man with black, and the stranger with the inhabitant of the land; and the place shall be holy" (p. 79). In contrast to this, after witnessing the events around Peter Halket's death, the Englishman who has been listening to the Colonials' talk decides that there is no justice in the moral world and "no God in Mashonaland" (p. 121). This perception is not contradicted. In fact, one of Schreiner's opening sequences in the narrative prophesies the bitter harvest of the imperial forces at work in the nineties. The scene alternates images of death and harvest, machine guns and reaping machines, and black men's heads and corn in sheaves. The image would be repeated in her best war story, "Eighteen-Ninety-Nine." As Alex La Guma has noted, the politics of Rhodes would become the politics of South Africa after union in 1910: legalized racism, labor exploitation, humiliation, brutalization of the nonwhite people, and their exclusion from political representation.[11] These were the favorable conditions that made South Africa "the hunting ground of international capitalism" (La Guma, 13). Schreiner shows these circumstances being laid down in Mashonaland, the "combination of racialism, capitalism and international imperialism (that) has made South Africa a colony of a special type" (La Guma, 13). As Oliver Tambo of the African National Congress put it, "the Europeans had the guns and were better organized" (La Guma, 18). Henceforth, the white man would be "baas."

Schreiner dedicated *Trooper Peter* to Sir George Grey, whom she admired as a truly civilizing and compassionate English administrator—and Rhodes's antithesis. This revelation emphasizes her duality as an English-South African. She still looked to England as the guarantor of her ideals of good government, even though all her writings of this period show her describing and representing the historical formation of an indigenous oppositional South African voice. There is a similar duality in her feminism: Maternity is still the sign under which her protest at white patriarchy functions although she was also forging a new feminist vision of the connecting links between imperialism and patriarchal attitudes. By unconsciously transposing into the narrative her own loss as a mother, she demonstrated that bodily experience and political protest are not separable: The crime of rape makes colonization felt in black women's bodies. In the narrative of Trooper Peter Halket's experiences in Mashonaland, the explicit effects and "the specific character of exploitation under capitalism" are discursively presented, and social structures and subjects are shown as interdependent practices.[12] "Olive Schreiner" is inscribed and transposed within her own decolonizing project at many levels. Despite her inevitable dualism—that of a white colonial English-speaking South African woman—she was right to be proud of having written *Trooper Peter Halket of Mashonaland*.

Closer Union

The best of Schreiner's qualities can be observed in her fluent and timely essays on immediate social conditions and political questions arising in South Africa at a crucial juncture: the turn of the nineteenth century. As Margaret Lenta points out in her new preface to *Thoughts on South Africa*, we see in these essays and pamphlets "the record of a powerful and disinterested mind" and of "a will to see through received prejudice into the facts of the case" (*TSA*, 6–7). Schreiner sums up current directions and conflicts, restates her own principles of equality, organicism, free growth, independence of spirit, and community service. Her analysis is flexible and open to evidence when she is in doubt on important issues. South Africa is seen comparatively, in relation to her own grasp of other colonies and political histories, and also as sui generis, evolving out of its own historical past.

Closer Union[13] has earned the consistent respect of posterity for its political foresight with regard to the relationship between forms of political organization and racial policy. The essay was written in October

1908, while the colonies were moving toward union and the new consti-
tution was being drafted by the National Convention for the Union.
Schreiner's argument was that federation would be more beneficial than
union, would be more cost effective, would prevent the tyranny of large
interests or individuals, and would produce a better civic spirit and better citizens. Federation would also enable the more liberal attitude of the
Cape toward the franchise to be built upon and extended rather than
abolished and would allow South Africa to evolve slowly toward being
"a free man's country" (*CU*, 8), rather than hastily assembled into a cen-
tralized Union benefiting capitalist interests and attitudes toward black
South Africans as a dehumanized labor resource. These views are pointedly expressed with practical good sense and respect for the principles of
a healthy polity, regional differences and specificity, and individual
rights.

Schreiner argues that everyone should have the federal franchise,
with no distinction of race or color. Within the regions there should be
an adult franchise with a demanding scholastic examination. Natives
still living under tribal tenure should elect a certain number of direct
representatives. An educational test would "serve as a stimulus in the
direction of education to both the poor whites and the natives" (*CU*, 6).
She argues that any attempt to base national life on distinctions of race
and color "will, after the lapse of many years, prove fatal to us" (*CU*, 8).
Interestingly, it was precisely the constant legislation and the attempt to
enforce educational policy on racial grounds that ushered in the last and
most destructive phase of civil struggle in South Africa in 1976.

As usual, Schreiner takes the long view and sees haste as self-destructive: "You cannot hurry South Africa and any attempt to do so may in
the long run make history repeat itself" (*CU*, 16). She is always in favor
of slow organic growth of loyalties and affiliations: Foundations should
be laid deep and well. She sees the "native question" as crucial, and
although she is apt to see the black man as the necessary laborer of
South Africa—"our vast laboring class"—that is what the current situation was. She points out the great social instincts and gifts of the African
from which whites could learn. She also asserts that class structure, in
which color difference coincides with class position, will one day be open
to change due to the process of education and a "free path" toward education, training, and citizenship (*CU*, 28). All of these principles would
be abandoned by the Union that was established in 1910. They were
even more ferociously violated after 1948, when the Nationalists came
to power and legislated racial segregation was allied with the infamous

policies of Bantu education. In one prophetic paragraph she warns against the cost of ignoring black rights to a healthy life and development:

> [I]f, blinded by the gain of the moment, we see nothing in our dark man but a vast engine of labor; if to us he is not a man, but only a tool; if dispossessed entirely of the land for which he now shows that large aptitude for peasant proprietorship for the lack of which among their masses many great nations are decaying; if we force him permanently in his millions into the locations and compounds and slums of our cities, obtaining his labor cheaper, but to lose what the wealth of five Rands could not return to us; if uninstructed in the highest forms of labor without the rights of citizenship, his own social organization broken up, without our having aided him to participate in our own; if, unbound to us by gratitude and sympathy, and alien to us in blood and colour, we reduce this mass to the condition of a great, seething, ignorant proletariat—then I would rather draw a veil over the future of this land. (*CU*, 29)

Against this astonishingly accurate prediction we now read the sorry, shameful history of disenfranchisement, forced removals, the Bantustan system, the conditions of the mine hostels, and the slum conditions of the urban townships that would eventually nurture the rebellions against intolerable exclusions and oppressions.

Furthermore, in this essay Schreiner reveals insight into the psychological effects on the white colonizer of living with a brutalized and feared colonized, the effects of anxiety, repression, and projection later so effectively analyzed by Otave Mannoni and Albert Memmi, analysts of the psychology of colonialism.[14] National existence would be lived in the shadow of fear; there would be "a crack down the entire height of the social structure"; a nemesis would follow: "[I]n the end the subjected people write their features on the face of the conquerors" (*CU*, 31). Racial discrimination would hinder the growth and development of white South Africans: "[T]he continual association with human creatures who are not free, will ultimately take from us our strength and our own freedom; and men will see in our faces the reflection of that on which we are always treading and looking down" (*CU*, 31).

She ends her essay with a plea for great leaders who would "lead our national conscience to shape itself in harmony with that ideal," the ideal of a wide justice and humanity. In *Closer Union* Schreiner reveals the great distance she had traveled from a dependence on England as the guarantor of a civilized society to a new form of patriotism forged during the sufferings of the Second Anglo-Boer War and in socialist resistance to the rise of capitalism in South Africa. The uitlander presence in the Transvaal and the alliances built up by Cecil Rhodes had taught her that only those who commit themselves to the future of a nation can be relied upon to act in its final best interests. In this essay she reveals her allegiance to thinkers like John Stuart Mill, whose book on political economy had been consigned to the flames by Tant Sannie for being the "devil's book." Decades of oppression, censorship, punishment, and death would follow for thinkers like Schreiner who expressed these views in the era about to follow the formation of the Union of South Africa, in which black South Africans were further disenfranchised. The constitutions currently being prepared and debated in the new South Africa resemble the blueprint Schreiner laid down almost 90 years ago.

Chapter Seven

Reentering Eden:
Woman and Labour

Schreiner always considered her ideas and writings connected with the crux of modernity and male-female relationships to be the core of her work, and everything she wrote has some bearing on this association. In the preface to *Woman and Labour,* she explains that a larger work she had completed on this topic had been destroyed when her house in Johannesburg was looted during the Anglo-Boer War. This fact was always passionately denied by her husband, S. C. Cronwright, and the material existence of this larger work became a point of contention between them and others. What the conflict revealed most clearly was that the outbreak of war was a personal as well as a national crux in Schreiner's life. It is probable that her marriage had for all intents and purposes ended, apart from a dispassionate friendship that continued.[1] Their union had suffered almost from the first by her need to follow where her health and asthma attacks dictated and from her husband's increasingly resentful expectation that she should finish her large books and earn their income since his income from farming had been removed. Whether their marriage went through the same phases of sexual mistrust and erosion as Frank and Rebekah's in *From Man to Man* it is difficult to say, but the pattern seems similar, with Schreiner's additional sensitivity to being a burden with her ill health and the physical stress of constant miscarriages in the nineties taking their toll. Whatever her personal anxiety, *Woman and Labour* is nevertheless a tough, sustained, and sometimes entertaining scrutiny of the effects of social changes on the intimate relationships of men and women at that time and a hope that the future would bring men and women closer together as they shared in labor and professional activity on a more equal basis.

Schreiner's feminism anticipates many of the elements of recent feminism in its attempt to attain a balance between acknowledging biological differences without falling into biological determinism. It also shares a desire to acknowledge the constraining effects of material conditions within society without destroying the felt agency and power of individual women. Her eloquently argued view is finely balanced around a sense of injustice at the exclusion of women from meaningful work in the world and at the unequal pay they received for the work they performed. Furthermore, it encompasses a sense that women as individuals and as the mothers of the race could do a great deal to change the social order that constrained their fulfillment and partnerships with men. Like her other pamphlets and sociopolitical essays, her method combines a rationalist structure in which views are advanced, objections posed and rebutted, and conclusions sketched with her preference for vivid and often domestic analogies, parables, African examples of birds and other creatures, and brief allegories. The rhetorical structure is cumulative—with repeated cries for "all labour as our province"—and ends on a visionary optimism for the "closer union" of new men and women in the future.

In the introduction Schreiner mentions the powerful effect on her of an African woman's portrait of their sufferings under polygamy and subjection, combined with an acceptance of their condition. As the essay develops, she tries to distinguish between this attitude and the one that underpinned the women's movement of her own time, "her conscious determination to modify her relation to life about her" (*TSA*, 182). In this respect *Woman and Labour* expands upon the argument Schreiner had presented in an earlier essay, "The Boer Woman and the Modern Woman's Question," in which her insights were comparatively stated in relation to Boer patterns of social life and behavior. In *Woman and Labour* she makes a larger attempt to give an evolutionary overview of the social changes that have curtailed women's traditional occupations, including their childbearing and child-rearing functions. In the introduction she advances the then revolutionary but now accepted view that society turned on women's unremunerated labor within the home and that attitudes toward housework should change. She mentions the women thrown into fields of new work who were nevertheless bound by conservative attitudes and customs. The injustice of unequal pay for equal work is stressed. She refers to the hope that equality of labor and economic independence would benefit sexual relationships and marriage, although "the present discoordinate transitional stage of our social growth" (*WL*, 8) might at times demand divorce. Here, too, her personal conflicts might have been taken up in a larger view of the social conditions with which many modern men and women were struggling. Conscious of her own representativeness within the stream of modernity, she was, as usual, seeking consolation for personal unhappiness. She understood that many thoughtful women were similarly beleaguered and that their suffering was no less intense than hers, although "primitive" women seemed to her more fatalistic.

In the first long chapter on parasitism, Schreiner locates this condition, her word for a state of passive dependence in any class—and she treats women as a class in this chapter—that loses its vital contributing role within any community or union. This chapter closely follows the argument in the essay on "The Boer Woman and the Modern Woman's Question," in which she perceives the women's movement as both new and conservative: "New, in that it is an attempt on the part of woman to adapt herself to conditions which have never existed before on the globe; conservative, in that it is an attempt to regain what she has lost" (*TSA,* 189), meaning her dignity as an equal laborer with men.

In the chapter on parasitism, she explains the changes that have been brought about by the industrial revolution and its different effects on women and men as skills and mental ability replaced muscular strength. She harps on the changes that have affected women materially, the modifications in methods of communication, and the differences between male and female unemployment or underemployment, with women losing whole fields of activity and given no new ones to replace them. Changes within domestic households and a decreased demand for fertility played a part in causing parasitism. Mighty armies of spinsters and prostitutes were changing the picture of women in society. Childbirth was becoming an "episodal occupation" rather than a life's work (*WL,* 26). Three-quarters of women's traditional activities had shrunk away—a statistic Schreiner called the "propelling force behind that vast and restless 'Woman's Movement' which marks our day" (pp. 26–27). What women were demanding, more or less articulately or instinctively, was their "share of honoured and socially useful human toil" (p. 27).

In the second section on parasitism, she elaborates on the different situations of male and female labor and compares conditions in different empires and civilizations. She also sketches the emergence of an inactive, economically dependent female class as a new, deplorable social phenomenon partly conditioned by the presence within the household of slaves or servants. Productive activity ceases for such materially pampered and enervated women who, if they bear children, also contribute to the enervation of the race. The real danger, she notes, is that such women, whether wives or prostitutes, become dependent on their passive sexual function alone. In the third section she looks more closely at class difference and notes that the condition of female workers is different from that of male laborers, whose interests are often best served by excluding women from their activities. The women's movement, she notes, has largely arisen within the educated middle classes and has different goals from those of the male labor unions, which seek further material rewards. In seeking further outlets for women's energies, the women's movement might not lead to any short-term material gains but rather to further struggle and suffering within "the new and continually unfolding material conditions" (p. 54). Carefully thought out in light of Schreiner's own experience and observations, these lucid distinctions are curiously modern in their emphasis on isolated struggle, materialism, and process as the conditions of feminist enterprise. Every individual woman's struggle thus becomes noble and valuable, a landmark in human evolution, even the small action that "resists the tyranny of fashions in dress or bearing or custom" (p. 55). Schreiner's feminism sees the crucial role of material conditions and the individual consciousness of woman as a site of daily struggle, a "primal battleground" (p. 62) where battles are fought and sometimes won. At the same time there has to be an "inter-evolution between the sexes" (p. 58) within the "readjustive sexual movement of today" (p. 58).

The women's movement is characterized as hybrid and organic, proceeding along different fronts and with varying levels of energy and appropriateness. It is precisely this apparently uncoordinated nature that reveals its authenticity, "showing how vital, spontaneous, and wholly organic and unartificial its nature is" (p. 61). Having broad and compelling social causes and manifesting a persistent, collaborative, and steady movement toward social change, the movement is both highly individualized and yet vaster than any individual: "I[I]t is through the labors of these myriad toilers, each working in her own minute sphere, with her own small outlook . . . that at last the widened and beautiful relations of women to life must rise, if they are ever to come" (p. 63). The movement is seen as directed toward posterity but drawing on the strength of the past, and Schreiner often calls up warrior figures, heroic strength, a "virile womanhood" that has both male and female attributes: "We are the daughters of our fathers as well as our mothers" (p. 65).

In her chapter on "Woman and War," Schreiner addresses the question of division of labor between the sexes. She expands on the point so graphically made by Lyndall in *The Story of an African Farm:* "If the bird does like its cage, and does like its sugar, and will not leave it, why keep the door so very carefully shut?" (p. 180). She argues in response to the hypothetical objection against women's entry into all possible fields of training and labor—that women are fitted for only certain kinds of work—that it is impossible to know, given the history of the subjection of women to the domestic sphere, which activities women are best suited to, or could perform well. Social history has made such knowledge impossible. Only if all fields of training and work are opened to women will it be possible to determine whether biological difference in itself is a limitation or determinant of work or capacity. In other words, nature will then decide, not men who have tended to reserve certain activities and professions for themselves. She explores the question of whether men and women really are best suited, as is often assumed, to abstract, scientific labor and nurturing physical labor respectively. She concludes that there are "no such natural and spontaneous divisions of labour based on natural sexual distinctions in the new fields of intellectual or delicately skilled manual labour, which are taking the place of the old" (p. 69). She leaves open the possibility, however, that future research on the brain may reveal certain capacities related to sexual difference. She deals satirically with the assumption from which she had herself no doubt suffered, that because many talented women write novels, there is some "inherent connection in the human brain between the ovarian sex function and the art of fiction" (p. 69). The truth is that modern fiction is the only art that can be exercised without special training or equipment and can be "produced in moments stolen from the multifarious, brain-destroying occupations which fill the average woman's life," thus encouraging a woman to turn to fiction by default, as it were. Here one hears the voice of the real married woman join with the impersonal construction of a feminist vision, partly contradicting her vision of herself as someone who would write, perforce, in order to express herself, even if she were alone on a star. In her mature polemic, thinking of constraints on women in society in general, Schreiner notices that the restrictions on women's training and activity are often used to damn them: Women who have only writing as an outlet can be castigated as silly women novelists. Thus she concludes that no organic connections can be proved between biological sex and professional aptitude: Women in contemporary society live in "crabbed, walled-in, and bound conditions" (p. 70).

As elsewhere in her letters, Schreiner emphasizes that current activities and occupations for men and women are not biologically determined but socially constructed. This is particularly evident in her footnote on the currently "unnatural method of sex clothing and dressing the hair," the exaggerated "visual differences" that do not relate to organic structural differences between the sexes but are "grotesque exaggerations of modern attire and artificial manners" (p. 71). Here she anticipates the modern feminist debates over the distorting socialization of the sexes. Given the state of partial knowledge concerning the relation between sexual structure and intellectual capacity, the women's movement demands "free trade in labour": "[N]atural conditions . . . should determine the labours of each individual" (p. 73). She cautions society not to tie a rope around a puppy's neck, figuratively speaking, and then "assert its incapacity to keep afloat!" A certain feminist irony had developed in Schreiner after decades of struggle and over a decade of marriage.

Schreiner asserts that arguments from biology and tradition should not be used to curtail the training and employment of women. Nevertheless, she also contends that in certain spheres of activity, such as war, biological capacity determines the difference in perspective between the sexes. Women have always played a role in war. However, quite apart from their courage in any past or future participation (she was no doubt thinking of the recent example of Boer women), the core of the matter is that women bear and rear children and thus have an intimate and indissoluble relation to war and killing: "We pay the first cost on all human life." The long months of pregnancy, the pain of childbirth, and the years spent in nurturing children mean that women can never look upon war and the casualties of war as men do. This is not because of any moral superiority or any loftier social instinct but because of a higher knowledge born of the flesh. This assertion suggests an intimate connection between—and a refusal to separate—the body and mental capacity or knowledge. A woman responds differently to hunting animals and the destruction of war; thus in this particular respect, they have a special insight to offer that should not be disregarded at a time that marks the birth of the modern world and its "crude disco-ordination of life on earth" (p. 78). She predicts that wars will cease when females share equally "in the control and government of modern national life" (p. 78).

In the next chapter Schreiner extends her double argument: that biological sex should not be used as a rationale for constraint, but where it does exert a determining difference, such differences should be valued and used in the construction of a healthy society. She argues again that the closer we approach the sphere of reproduction, the more a difference, a "certain distinct psychic attitude," is inclined to appear (p. 85). The activity and the wider contribution that women can make from this distinct psychic attitude make them important both individually and as a class. Here Schreiner anticipates the recent research of Carol Gilligan, *In a Different Voice.*[2] Elsewhere she calls this different capacity "a kind of secondary sexual characteristic" endowed upon women by a mixture of biology and traditional occupation: "long years of servitude and physical subjection, and her experience as child-bearer and protector of infancy" (p. 96). This is obviously in spite of the fact that many women do not experience childbirth. This view of the relationship between nature and nurture is finely nuanced and leaves room for the accountability of social training and custom, the choices women make, and the significance of biological difference. It also has implications for law and judicial areas: She points out that men should not represent women in adjudicating matters such as the legalization of prostitution, claims to child custody, and which forms of infidelity constitute grounds for divorce. This is a narrow region where "sex as sex" manifestly plays its part (p. 87). Schreiner's argument greatly predates contemporary struggles by feminists to have the social impact of sexual difference recognized within the judicial process.

The next phase of her argument tackles the icon of the "divine child-bearer" and ironically portrays the ways in which it has been manipulated to suit male and class interests. Those men most apt to use the "divine childbearer" role to keep women out of professional spheres are also those least apt to acknowledge this figure outside their own class and daily practice. The theorist at the fireside, she declares, is less than apt to exclaim to his household drudge: "Divine Childbearer! Potential mother of the race! Why should you clean my boots or bring my tea, while I lie warm in bed? Is it not enough that you should have the holy and mysterious power of bringing the race to life? Be contented. Henceforth I shall get up at dawn and make my own tea and pay you just the same!" (p. 90).

She points out that it is the economic reward that lies at the core of the resistance to divine childbearers entering male occupations. Men are mostly content for women to be baby-sitters, tea pickers, and washerwomen; it is when they threaten their own occupations that specious arguments are advanced.

The question as to whether women have sufficient capacity to enter all fields of future training and employment as equals Schreiner answers in a spate of allegory and rhetorical flight. A woman mountain climber, counterpart to the male hunter of her earlier allegory, climbs a steep mountain in Switzerland, bearing cattle fodder, the "archetype of the mighty labouring woman" (p. 98). In another parable many theorists stand around a bird hatched from a found egg and speculate about its identity: Is it a waterfowl, a barnyard fowl, a parrot, or perhaps a bird capable of great flight? The bird, meanwhile, has a leg chained to a log. Should they set it free? The bird looks up at the sky, "the sky, in which it had never yet been set free—for the bird knew what it would do. It was an eaglet" (p. 100). Similarly, women know what they can do and also comprehend exactly where artificial constraints limit their capacities.

The final objection to women's emancipation that Schreiner counters is that sexual attraction and capacity will be diminished if women are highly educated and trained. She counters this objection by arguing, first, that money is always enticing in a mate! Second, freedom in a mate is often an attraction and confers high value. She cites highly intelligent women in history, such as George Sand, who attracted notable men, even when middle aged and rolling "cigarettes in a dingy office" (p. 105). Further training would in fact free unions from "the sex purchasing power of the male" (p. 108), on which they have previously been too dependent. Only feeble men, who like their women to be materially dependent on them, would be the losers. Marriage would no longer be "some form of sexual sale" (p. 110). Everyone would benefit by there being two potential breadwinners in a family. Prostitution, in its broadest sense, which covers all unions in which sexual functions are exchanged for material goods, would become extinct. The "economic freedom and social independence of women" would not exterminate sexual love between men and women; rather, it would "fully 'enfranchise' " it. This point is nobly and persuasively presented and is the core of Schreiner's mature feminism: "Sexual love, after its long pilgrimage in the deserts, would be enabled to return at last, a sovereign crowned" (p. 111).

The women's movement, then, is characterized not by an opposition to men but by a movement "of the sexes towards closer union" (p. 114). The link with the title of her political pamphlet on South Africa reveals her allegiance, in thinking about politics and marriage, to fundamental principles of individual freedom and autonomy, slow growth, and equal, uncoerced association. This leads into her last section on "The New Woman and the New Man" as "the two sides of a coin cast in one mould" (p. 117). Marriage would become a new companionship under new conditions. Why, then, was there at the time such "pain, unrest, and sexual disco-ordination"? This Schreiner sees as part of a process of general upheaval at the birth of modernity, at a time of rapid evolution and change. Conflicting ideals and institutions that cause widespread human suffering are produced by vastly revised material conditions in industrialized society utilizing mechanical labor, the wide dissemination of knowledge through the printing press, urbanization, and internationalization and contact with other cultures. This occurs within families, marriages, and individuals, and its complexity is truly conveyed only within art, "where actual concrete individuals are shown acting and reacting on each other" (p. 123). The expression of her own feminism leads Schreiner to define the problem novel of her day and of her practice, the novel that persistently deals with "subtle social problems, religious, sexual and political" (p. 124) because the artist must portray "that which lies at the core of its life" (p. 124). Solitude and suffering, which were increasingly Schreiner's own lot, would be the mark of the leader. The social disharmony of the age were most keenly felt in sexual matters because in the region of sex we touch "the spinal cord of human existence" (p. 125). The best marriages of the future would often be based on shared professional concerns as well as sexual attraction. Common impersonal sympathies would maintain vitality and interest in unions between men and women.

In a visionary epilogue, Schreiner movingly creates epic figures of this new, equal union, one that in her own personal life was becoming a thing of the past. Figures stand with shaded eyes gazing into the future at the beginning of a new century. In our dreams we hear the last turn of the key closing the last brothel. "As we row against the stream of life," visionary figures of harmony appear in "a clear, a golden light" (p. 131). We glimpse a nobler future in which men and women work hand in hand in "an Eden created by their own labour and made beautiful by their own fellowship." This glorious new age could come into being only if the cry of contemporary women were heard: "Give us labour and the training that fits us for labour!" (p. 132).

In *Woman and Labour* a strong materialist feminism is brought into play with a visionary futurism that alone could transform individual suffering and disharmony into social progress. Although Schreiner is always aware of her historical position as a spokesperson, her sophisticated arguments often have a contemporary ring. *Woman and Labour* is a seamless whole punctuated by the cry of her age. Many of the conditions she predicted have been brought about. The feminist consciousness she was struggling to bring into being is now widespread in many societies. She was addressing herself both to the conditions of her own time, uncovering their deep causes, and to the posterity that would look back with amazement at what was not obvious to Schreiner and her contemporaries.

Her essay is a model of lucidity, often rising into surges of visionary rhetoric that were meant to be, and that often are, inspirational. She was faithful to the hybrid nature of feminism as a material struggle within particular historical conditions and as a visionary source of inspiration to the women who followed. In 1913, two years after the publication of *Woman and Labour*, as if her task were done, she left her husband and South Africa and departed for England, ostensibly on a quest for better medical treatment and health.

That same year, the Land Act was passed in South Africa, perhaps the single most consequential piece of legislation affecting black life in that country. It created a homeless proletariat, poverty, desperation, and a system of migrant labor that would effectively shatter black family life; at this same time, Schreiner dreamed her long-term dream of the equal union of the sexes in a resplendent future.[3] In the previous year the South African Native National Congress (later the ANC) was founded, and the countermovement was instigated that would finally right the racial power imbalance in South Africa. The coincidence of these dates underlines the fact that an era had passed, an era within which Schreiner was a founder of the best strain of liberalism, a form of liberalism adapted to South African conditions and one that began to articulate the connections between forms of oppression. The aspect of racial injustice that was muted or subliminal in her work would subsequently become a central focus of South African political struggle and art as the noose of racial oppression tightened.

World War I (1914–1918) confirmed both her pacifism and her outsider position as a woman with a German name living in London. After lonely years in England, she returned to South Africa in August 1919 and died peacefully—spectacles and book in hand—in a Cape Town boardinghouse on the night of December 10, 1920. In one of her last letters she wrote: "It doesn't seem to me this is Africa" (*CB*, 132).

Schreiner's strength lay in the deep roots she had in a preindustrial South Africa and in the ways in which she attempted to make her striving, idealistic vision, nourished in those landscapes, relevant to an emergent, urban, capitalistic culture. The vigor of her feminism lies in its close ties to her personal experience, her ability to depersonalize and conceptualize that experience, her monumental vision of a future that she cast into strongly rhetorical prose for other women, and the principle of an ideal social justice to which she remained loyal. *The Story of an African Farm* lives on as a sharply etched yet dreamy classic, endlessly mutating into new forms for new phases of South African life.

Schreiner's wide-ranging erudition and her poignant emotional needs make her an affectionately regarded, recognizable woman intellectual. Her attempt to be fully alive to her own era, to respond adequately to the place and time in which she lived, has made her an ineradicable part of the history of South Africa, a history in which oppression and resistance have been complex and intertwined. One of the best tributes to her pervasive "vitalising influence," which extended far beyond the country of her birth, was paid by Vera Brittain, who commented on her perception of "the complex interaction of the different struggles for human freedom, and the fundamental identity of violence in war with the social violence which overwhelms all the victims of power."[4]

Notes and References

Preface

    1. Vera Buchanan-Gould, *Not without Honour: The Life and Writings of Olive Schreiner* (London: Hutchinson, 1948).

    2. Richard Rive, ed., *Olive Schreiner Letters 1871–1899* (Cape Town: David Philip, 1989), 370; hereafter cited in text.

    3. Marion V. Friedmann, *Olive Schreiner: A Study in Latent Meanings* (Johannesburg: Witwatersrand University Press, 1955).

    4. Ruth First and Ann Scott, *Olive Schreiner* (London: Deutsch, 1980); hereafter cited in text as First.

    5. Kathleen Blake, *Love and the Woman Question in Victorian Literature: The Art of Self-Postponement* (Sussex: The Harvester Press, 1983).

    6. Charles Darwin's extended exploratory voyages of 1831–36, including a visit to the Cape, led to *The Origin of Species* (1859), which set forth his theory of evolution through the transmutation of species. In South Africa there was strong opposition to Darwin's theories, represented in Schreiner's *The Story of an African Farm* by the literal-minded theology of Tant Sannie, and Em. Schreiner read Darwin's *Descent of Man* in 1873 and his *Variations of Animals and Plants* in 1875–76. Darwin's thought and style permeate Schreiner's themes and tropes, especially her imagery of mutation and evolutionary progression through adaptive variation. See Karel Schoeman's *Olive Schreiner: A Woman in South Africa:1855–1881* (Johannesburg: Jonathan Ball, 1991), 137–38; hereafter cited in text.

    7. Doris Lessing, afterword to *The Story of an African Farm* (New York: Fawcett, 1968).

    8. Schreiner's own formulations on this issue—the paradoxical loss and gain of "self" experienced in the process of writing—anticipates the recent complex debates in poststructuralist thought. See, for example, responses to the idea of self and political responsibility in South Africa in David Attwell's interviews with South African novelist J. M. Coetzee, David Attwell, ed. *Doubling the Point: Essays and Interviews* (Cambridge: Harvard University Press, 1992). The discussion is also developed by Peter Horn in a review of *Doubling the Point,* "Imagining the Unimaginable," *Southern African Review of Books* 5, no. 3 (May/June 1993): 14–15, and by my review article, "White Writing and Postcolonial Politics," *Ariel* 25, no.4 (October 1994): 153–67.

    9. Rachel Blau Du Plessis, *Writing Beyond the Ending: Narrative Strategies of Twentieth Century Women Writers* (Bloomington: Indiana University Press, 1985).

10.   Christina Barsby, "Olive Schreiner: Towards a Redefinition of Culture," *Pretexts: Studies in Literature and Culture* 1, no.1 (Winter 1989): 18–39.

11.   Joyce Avrech Berkman, *The Healing Imagination of Olive Schreiner: Beyond South African Colonialism,* (Amherst: University of Massachusetts Press, 1989), hereafter cited in text.

12.   Gerald Monsman, *Olive Schreiner's Fiction: Landscape and Power* (New Brunswick, N.J.: Rutgers University Press, 1991), 15; hereafter cited in text.

13.   See Gerald Monsman, "Olive Schreiner's Allegorical Vision," *Victorian Review* 18, no. 2 (Winter 1992): 49–63, and Irene Gorak, "Olive Schreiner's Colonial Allegory: *The Story of an African Farm,*" *Ariel* 23, no. 4 (October 1992): 53–72, both hereafter cited in text.

14.   Olive Schreiner, "The Dawn of Civilization. Stray Thoughts on Peace and War. The Homely Personal Confessions of a Believer in Human Unity," *The Nation and Athenaeum* (26 March 1921): 912–14; 913; hereafter cited as "Dawn."

15.   Juliet Mitchell and Jacqueline Rose, *Feminine Sexuality: Jacques Lacan and the école freudienne* (New York: W. W. Norton, 1985).

16.   See Anne McClintock," Olive Schreiner: The Limits of Colonial Feminism," in *Imperial Leather: Race, Gender and Sexuality in the Colonial Context* (London: Routledge, 1995), 258–95, 267.

17.   Malvern van Wyk Smith, *Grounds of Contest: A Survey of South African English Literature* (Cape Town: Juta, 1990), 2.

Chapter One

1.   S. C. Cronwright-Schreiner, *The Life of Olive Schreiner* (London: Fisher-Unwin, 1924), 69; hereafter cited as SCCS, *Life.*

2.   S. C. Cronwright-Schreiner, *The Letters of Olive Schreiner: 1876–1920* (London: Fisher-Unwin, 1924), 287; hereafter cited as SCCS, *Letters.*

3.   Olive Schreiner, *The Story of an African Farm* (Johannesburg: Ad. Donker, 1986), 176; hereafter cited in text as *SAF.*

4.   See Nancy Chodorow, *The Reproduction of Mothering: Psychoanalysis and the Sociology of Gender* (Berkeley: University of California Press, 1978) and Dorothy Dinnerstein, *The Mermaid and the Minotaur* (New York: Harper and Row, 1976).

5.   In the penultimate chapter of *African Farm,* Waldo's dream is described as "new-tinted": "Our fathers had their dreams; we have ours; the generation that follows will have its own" (*SAF,* 271–2).

6.   Letter to W. P. Schreiner, 22 March 1907, UCT Collection.

7.   See Havelock Ellis's "Notes on Olive Schreiner," HRHRC Collection, University of Texas, Austin, Texas.

8.   Anne McClintock argues that when the white mother figure is redeemed into purity, punitive authority is displaced onto the black "ayah" or servant, as in *From Man to Man* (269–70).

9. Olive Schreiner, *From Man to Man* (London: Virago, 1982), 43–44; hereafter cited in text as *FMM*.

10. Jane Rendall, *The Origins of Modern Feminism: Women in Britain, France and the United States, 1780–1860* (Chicago: Lyceum Books, 1985), 107; hereafter cited in text.

11. See Schreiner's "Lily Kloof" journal entry for 21 November 1880: "Horrible desire for immortality last night; hope I shall die suddenly. Anything else is easily given up for truth—but immortality." Journal extracts reprinted in *Olive Schreiner*, ed. Cherry Clayton (Johannesburg: McGraw-Hill, 1983), 106; hereafter cited in text as *CB*.

12. Olive Schreiner, "Diamond Fields" manuscript, published by Richard Rive in *English in Africa* 1, no.1 (March 1974): 3–29, 24; cited as "DF."

13. Letter to Karl Pearson, Rive, *Letters*, 65. Schreiner's concern with prostitution was lifelong and crucial to her understanding of women's liberation and equality. It affected the social concern she developed in London, her views on the double standard of sexual behavior, the relationship between the exchange of women for wealth and their subordinate social status, the behavior of male prostitutes who were never termed prostitutes (thus a feminist understanding of language), and the way in which prostitutes functioned in society as guardians of domestic virtue.

14. The Gau incident is fully discussed by Karel Schoeman (1992: 222–28). It seems likely that Schreiner either was pregnant or believed herself to be after one or more sexual incidents with Gau. One researcher, however, has also recently argued that she probably was pregnant and experienced a first miscarriage/abortion, given the overwhelming fictional concern with pregnancy and lost or dead babies and the evidence of unconscious textuality and language usage as well as the agonizing recurrence of episodes of sexual and social scandal in her life. See Helen Bradford, Department of History, University of Cape Town, "Sex, Secrets, and Olive Schreiner: Fact and Fiction," unpublished paper. The feminist significance of Schreiner's fictional concern with illegitimacy, pregnancy, and maternity lies in her emphasis on the more grievous consequences of sexuality and social codes for women than for men. For women, the risk of pregnancy is real and is often carried alone or becomes a trap. The Gau incident was traumatic for Schreiner because of the secrecy that enshrouded the relationship, the discrepancy between sexual passion and social codes of conduct at a Wesleyan manse, the shock of the broken engagement, and probably the shock of a miscarriage or abortion. She traced her bitterness about relationships with men to this early incident.

15. Rodney Davenport, *A Modern History of South Africa* (Johannesburg: Macmillan, 1978), 26.

16. Olive Schreiner, *Thoughts on South Africa* (London: Fisher Unwin, 1923). The edition referred to is *Thoughts on South Africa*, ed. Margaret Lenta (Johannesburg: Ad. Donker, 1992), 18.

17. See Schreiner's preface to *Woman and Labour* (London: Fisher Unwin, 1911) ; references are to *Woman and Labour*, ed. Jane Graves (London: Virago, 1978), hereafter cited in text. See also Schreiner's incomplete preface to Mary Wollstonecraft's *A Vindication of the Rights of Woman*, MS fragment, National English Literary Museum Collection, hereafter cited as "MW."

18. Kenneth Clark, *Provincialism*, English Association Presidential Address (London: np, 1962), 9.

Chapter Two

1. Elaine Showalter, *Sexual Anarchy: Gender and Culture at the Fin de Siècle* (London: Blooomsbury, 1991), 3; hereafter cited in text.

2. Ann L. Ardis, *New Women, New Novels: Feminism and Early Modernism* (New Brunswick: Rutgers University Press, 1990), 3; hereafter cited in text.

3. Karl Pearson, "Woman and Labour," *Fortnightly Review* 129 (May 1984): 561, quoted by Showalter, 7.

4. This is the thesis of Ann Ardis in her *New Women, New Novels: Feminism and Early Modernism*. She points out that over a hundred novels were written about the "New Woman" between 1883 and 1900 and that they have been neglected for specific reasons that have to do with the politics of cultural explanations. Such New Woman novels have been marginalized by contemporary feminist critics as well as by modernists (Ardis, 4–7).

5. Patricia Stubbs, *Women and Fiction: Feminism and the Novel, 1880–1920* (London: Harvester Press, 1979), 115; hereafter cited in text.

6. Nancy Armstrong, *Desire and Domestic Fiction: A Political History of the Novel* (New York: Oxford University Press, 1987), 8–9; hereafter cited in text.

7. Hardy's *Tess of the D'Urbervilles* was originally subtitled "A Pure Woman," and Schreiner constantly emphasizes Bertie's innocence and purity. Patricia Stubbs suggests that Tess "shows us just how unnatural the bourgeois notion of sexuality really was, especially female sexuality" (67).

8. Olive Schreiner, *Undine* (New York: Harper & Brothers, 1928), 170; hereafter cited in text as *Undine*.

9. Leslie Rabine, *Reading the Romantic Heroine: Text, History, Ideology* (Ann Arbor: University of Michigan Press, 1987), 8; hereafter cited in text.

10. Sandra M. Gilbert and Susan Gubar, *The Madwoman in the Attic: The Woman Writer and the Nineteenth Century Literary Imagination* (New Haven: Yale University Press, 1979), 45–92.

11. See, for instance, Nina Auerbach's essay, "Engorging the Patriarchy," in *Feminist Issues in Literary Scholarship*, ed. Shari Benstock (Bloomington: Indiana University Press, 1987), 150–60. Auerbach argues that women have used writing to "possess forbidden experiences, forbidden knowledge, forbidden powers" and that women's ideologies have been "less pure than passionate because they reflect the humiliations and the compromised victories of all of our lives" (159).

12.   Mark Spilka, "On the Enrichment of Poor Monkeys by Myth and Dream; or, How Dickens Rousseauisticized and pre-Freudianized Victorian Views of Childhood," in *Sexuality and Victorian Literature*, ed. D. R. Cox (Knoxville: University of Tennessee Press, 1984), 165; hereafter cited in text.

13.   Schreiner gave a copy of Stowe's *Uncle Tom's Cabin* as a prize to one of her pupils at Ratel Hoek farm on May 5, 1877 (SCCS, *Life*, 130), so presumably she had read it herself while working on her own novels, or earlier.

14.   Schreiner included both Charlotte and Emily Brontë in her 1888 list of the world's twelve greatest women and considered Emily perhaps the "greatest woman of genius the English-speaking peoples had produced" (SCCS, *Life*, 181). It is likely that she had read more of Dickens and the Brontës before leaving South Africa than she mentions, as she speaks of rereading *Oliver Twist* in 1915 (SCCS, *Letters*, 353) and uses *Barnaby Rudge* as an instance of the simplicity, vividness, and directness of Dickens's art of fiction (SCCS, *Letters*, 363). Schreiner is often compared with Emily Brontë in terms of her passionate response to, and vivid re-creation of, a particular regional landscape.

15.   Jane P. Tompkins, "Sentimental Power: *Uncle Tom's Cabin* and the Politics of Literary History," in *The New Feminist Criticism: Essays on Women, Literature, and Theory*, ed. Elaine Showalter (London: Virago, 1986), 81–104, 83, 84, 85; hereafter cited in text.

16.   Havelock Ellis often mentioned to Schreiner her indebtedness to her "ancestral preaching Lyndalls . . . like the charnel house medieval ideas" that lived on in Marlowe, Shakespeare, and Webster. See Yaffa Claire Draznin, *My Other Self: The Letters of Olive Schreiner and Havelock Ellis, 1884–1920* (New York: Peter Lang, 1992), 244–45; hereafter cited in text. This is the most scholarly edition of the Schreiner-Ellis correspondence, and I have used it as a preferred reference when a letter citation exists in this volume. A useful source of basic information on people and places in Schreiner's life, it also contextualizes their correspondence.

17.   Dorothy Driver, "Women and Nature, Women as Objects of Exchange: Towards a Feminist Analysis of South African Literature," in *Perspectives on South African English Literature*, eds. Michael Chapman, Colin Gardner, and Es'kia Mphahlele (Johannesburg: Ad. Donker, 1992), 454–74, 467–68.

18.   Susan Brown, "A Victorian Sappho: Agency, Identity, and The Politics of Poetics," *English Studies in Canada* 20, no. 2 (June 1994): 205–25, 207.

19.   Anne McClintock, "Maidens, Maps and Mines: *King Solomon's Mines* and the Reinvention of Patriarchy in Colonial South Africa," in *Women and Gender in Southern Africa to 1945,* ed. Cherryl Walker (Cape Town: David Philip, 1990), 98.

20.   In Schreiner's sexual case history, documented amongst others by Havelock Ellis, her friend and confidant, she described how the erotic daydreams of her girlhood evolved into love stories of which she was the heroine. See Ellis's *Studies in the Psychology of Sex* (Philadelphia: Davis, 1929), vol. 3, Appendix B, History 9. The correspondence between Ellis and Schreiner in

1884–85, annotated by Draznin, reveals the intimacy and frankness of their discussion of sexuality, both in itself and in relation to social reform.

21.   Schreiner's friend Mary Brown described finding her hiding under the table in her London rooms to avoid visitors. Her husband, Samuel Cronwright, described his first impression of her in the same terms: She "had a shy, nervous look like a wild creature when she met strangers" (*Life*, 233).

22.   Showalter describes the interconnection between the three-decker novel, circulating libraries, Victorian decorum, and censorship: "But the death of the three-decker was primarily economic and followed a decision by the lending libraries in 1894. From 193 triple-decker novels published in 1884, the number dropped to merely four by 1897" (16). Schreiner's refusal to temper any of the nonconformist details of her fiction was an early form of the resistance to censorship that later South African writers were also compelled to practice.

23.   See Carol Barash, "Virile Womanhood: Olive Schreiner's Narratives of a Master Race," in *Speaking of Gender* (New York: Routledge, 1989), 269–281, regarding some of these contradictions. Also see Joyce Berkman, "The Nurturant Fantasies of Olive Schreiner," *Frontiers* 2, no. 3 (1977): 8–17.

24.   Schreiner described writing this singular scene to Ellis (Draznin, 243); Schoeman notes that Schreiner constructed a similar scene for the "Shabby Woman" who loves a married man in *Undine* and loves to touch his brushes and clothes (313).

25.   See Helen Bradford, "Introducing Palinsky Smith," *English in Africa* 21, nos. 1 and 2 (July 1994): 1–32. Bradford's discussion and this short story, first printed in Fred Schreiner's school publication, *The New College Magazine*, illuminate Schreiner's constant satirical concern with the "ignorant imperialist" in Africa (Bradford, 8) and the "superior but financially embarrassed Englishman" (10) who reinvents patriarchy in the colonies. He could take different forms (Harry Blair in *Undine*; Gregory Rose in *African Farm*) but was based on the English social reality of impoverished younger sons like Rider Haggard or consumptive sons sent to Africa for their health, like Cecil Rhodes. What Bradford calls the "dissolution of male fictions as they collide with colonial facts" (13) would be explored further in *Trooper Peter Halket of Mashonaland*.

26.   Loralee MacPike, "The Fallen Woman's Sexuality: Childbirth and Censure," in *Sexuality and Victorian Literature*, ed. D. R. Cox (Knoxville: University of Tennessee Press, 1984), 54–71, 61; hereafter cited in text.

27.   Schoeman discusses colonial attitudes to the "half-civilized" black man at the Diamond Fields (259–63). Schreiner's contemptuous treatment of the "not half-civilized" colonial "nigger" in *Undine* (281) reveals how enmeshed she was in the white South African attitude that aimed to "civilize" blacks but treated Westernized behavior and dress with humor or scorn. Michael Wade argues that a passage in *Undine* delineating racial types at the Fields (281) displays a syntactic confusion that reflects "an intense emotional involvement in the act of classification" and a European intellectual taxonomy. See Michael

Wade, "Adamastor's Mighty Shade," in *White on Black in South Africa: A Study of English-Language Inscriptions of Skin Colour* (London: Macmillan, 1993), 2–3.

28. Freud traces the different male and female forms taken by the "phantasy" entitled "A Child is Being Beaten" as "A Contribution to the Study of the Origin of Sexual Perversions" in *The Complete Psychological Works of Sigmund Freud* ([London: The Hogarth Press, 1955] vol. 17, 175–204). Freud discusses the different forms the fantasy can take—repression, sadism, and masochism—and posits a theory that "the nucleus of the unconscious (that is to say, the repressed) is in each human being that side of him which belongs to the opposite sex" (201). In Waldo's flogging scene, then, we would see the "return of the repressed," in that a boy child is beaten by a harsh surrogate father, one who ousts a gentle father figure. Freud traces three phases for the girl child, the third of which always has a boy being beaten by someone from "the class of fathers" (196). It is noteworthy, given Freud's tracing of libido and guilt, that Lyndall comforts Waldo by kissing him, thus uniting infantile boy and girl selves in an act of compassion and healing.

Chapter Three

1. Schreiner described the massive and wide-ranging response to her novel at the time of publication, when letters came "from all classes of people, from an Earl's son to a dressmaker in Bond Street, and from a coalheaver to a poet" (Rive, *Letters*, 109). *African Farm* was seen rather patronizingly as a first work of genius (by people like Sir Charles Dilke) to emerge from a British colony (Rive, *Letters*, 172). In South Africa its impact has been wide-ranging, diffusive, and enduring, a seminal text constantly refashioned by writers as various as Bessie Head, William Plomer, Nadine Gordimer, J. M. Coetzee, and Peter Wilhelm.

2. J. M. Coetzee, *Age of Iron* (London: Penguin, 1990), 106.

3. See letter from Olive Schreiner to W. P. Schreiner, October 1918, UCT collection.

4. See Graham Pechey, "*The Story of an African Farm* and the Discontinuous Text," *Critical Arts* 3, no.1: 65–78 and A. E. Voss, "A generic approach to the South African Novel in English," *UCT Studies in English* 7 (September 1977): 110–121.

5. See Gary Boire, "Transparencies: Of Sexual Abuse, Ambivalence, and Resistance," *Essays on Canadian Writing* 51–52 (Winter 1993–Spring 1994): 211–32. Boire's argument that male imperialism defines "the (sexed) child-body as a colonial space" (230) illuminates Schreiner's constant linkage of child abuse and colonialism. Scenes like Waldo's beating are not more excessive than the colonial practices of forced labor so endemic and crucial in the construction and maintenance of the South African state and the violence used to maintain that unenfranchised labor force.

6. Jenny Sharpe, *Allegories of Empire: The Figure of Woman in the Colonial Text.* (Minneapolis: University of Minnesota Press, 1993), 28.

7. See Tony Voss, "Avatars of Waldo," *Alternation* 1, no. 2 (1994): 15–25, who restates the case for forms of transcendence in responses to *African Farm* over time: "If Olive Schreiner's Waldo is a congener of Blackburn's black hero and heroine, Jochem van Bruggen's Ampie, Dhlomo's Robert Zulu, and Abrahams' Xuma, then literature may be able to give us, at a time when we need it, access to experience beyond our limitations of gender, race, and class" (25). The deconstruction of unitary identity within intertextuality becomes a liberating practice.

8. Ruth Parkins-Gounelas, *Fictions of the Female Self: Charlotte Brontë, Olive Schreiner, Katherine Mansfield* (London: Macmillan, 1991), 77.

9. Judith Kegan Gardiner, cited in Sandra M. Gilbert and Susan Gubar, *No Man's Land: The Place of the Woman Writer in the Twentieth Century,* vol. 2, *Sexchanges* (New Haven: Yale University Press, 1989), 66.

10. Gerd Bjorhovde, *Rebellious Structures: Women Writers and the Crisis of the Novel: 1880–1900* (Oslo: Norwegian University Press, 1987), 21–58 and Parkins-Gounelas, 81–82.

11. See my comparative discussion of Schreiner and Mansfield and female creativity in exile, "Olive Schreiner and Katherine Mansfield: Artistic Transformation of the Outcast Figure by Two Colonial Women Writers" in *Short Fiction in the New Literatures in English,* ed. Jacqueline Bardolph (Nice: Faculté des Lettres, 1989), 31–40.

12. See Robin Visel, " 'We Bear the World and We Make It': Bessie Head and Olive Schreiner," *Research in African Literatures* 21, no. 3 (Fall 1990): 115–124.

Chapter Four

1. See Jean Marquard, "Olive Schreiner's 'Prelude': The Child as Artist," *English Studies in Africa* 22, no. 1 (March 1979): 1–11.

2. Laura E. Donaldson, *Decolonizing Feminisms: Race, Gender, and Empire-Building* (Chapel Hill: University of North Carolina Press, 1992), 132–35.

3. Ellis records Schreiner's comments on this relationship at Ventnor, just after she had left her brother's house at Eastbourne, shortly after her arrival in England. She seems to have felt great attraction and fear simultaneously for this unidentified lover. She told Ellis, "quite calmly," that she wanted him to "tread on me and stamp me fine into powder." She waited for a promised visit from him, made herself a new dress, ate, and took quinine "in order to be well and strong for him," but he never came. This reads like a short story of which she was the heroine, perhaps a Gothic romance, and also testifies to the contradictory nature of her sexual attraction to men. Ellis's own interest in pathology may well have influenced the style of Schreiner's confessions to him. See Draznin's edition of the correspondence and editorial comment on this relationship as it partly shaped Schreiner's style of communication.

4. Anthony Voss, *"From Man to Man*: Heroic Fragment," in *The Flawed Diamond: Essays on Olive Schreiner,* ed. Itala Vivan (Sydney: Dangaroo Press, 1989), 135–145, 144. See Stephen Gray's "The Frontier Myth and the

Hottentot Eve," in his *Southern African Literature: An Introduction* (Cape Town: David Philip, 1979), 38–71.

5. Jeff Guy argues that the foundations of the "history of participation and resistance to dominance" in South Africa will be found in South Africa's precapitalist societies, "where women's labour and women's fertility, though appropriated by men, still provided the bedrock upon which these societies were built." See Jeff Guy, "Gender Oppression in Precapitalist Societies," in *Women and Gender in Southern Africa to 1945,* ed. Cherryl Walker (Cape Town: David Philip, 1990), 33–47, 47.

Chapter Five

1. Judith R. Walkowitz, "Science, Feminism and Romance: The Men and Women's Club, 1885–1889," *History Workshop Journal* 21 (Spring 1986): 37–59.

2. W. T. Stead, "The Maiden Tribute of Modern Babylon," *Pall Mall Gazette* (July 1885). Stead was editor of the journal, and his campaign was aimed at publicizing the Criminal Law Amendment Bill, which raised the age of consent for young women. The bill was first introduced in 1863 and was in danger of being dropped in 1885.

3. Olive Schreiner, *Dreams* (London: Fisher Unwin, 1890), 128; hereafter cited in text.

4. See Wilson Harris, "Comedy and Modern Allegory: A Personal View," in *A Shaping of Connections: Commonwealth Literature Studies—Then and Now,* eds. Hena Maes-Jelinek, Kirsten Holst Petersen, and Anna Rutherford (Sydney: Dangaroo Press, 1989), 127–140, and Harris's other critical writings.

5. Laura E. Donaldson, *Decolonizing Feminisms: Race, Gender and Empire-Building* (Chapel Hill: University of North Carolina Press, 1992), 133; hereafter cited in text. Donaldson is quoting here from Teresa de Lauretis, *Alice Doesn't: Feminism, Semiotics, Cinema* (Bloomington: Indiana University Press, 1984), 77.

Chapter Six

1. Patrick Brantlinger, "Victorians and Africans: The Genealogy of the Myth of the Dark Continent," in *"Race," Writing, and Difference,* ed. Henry Louis Gates Jr. (Chicago: University of Chicago Press, 1986), 185–222, 191; hereafter cited in text.

2. See Sally-Ann Murray's new introduction to Olive Schreiner, *Trooper Peter Halket of Mashonaland,* 1897 (Johannesburg: Ad. Donker, 1992).

3. The full quotation reads: "What we really suffer from is the fact that man believes there is quite one moral law in sexual matters for himself and another for woman. If he respected woman more, if he felt she was his equal in the eye of the law, with the same powers and right[s], he would cease to think that what would be absolutely wicked degraded vice in a woman, is quite

noble, and right in himself!" Letter to Fan Schreiner, 12 June 1908, UCT Collection, quoted in *Olive Schreiner*, ed. Cherry Clayton (Johannesburg: McGraw-Hill, 1983), 126.

4. Olive Schreiner, *An English-South African's View of the Situation: Words in Season* (London: Hodder & Stoughton, 1899); hereafter cited in text.

5. See Ronald Robinson, John Gallagher, and Alice Denny, *Africa and the Victorians: The Official Mind of Imperialism* (London: MacMillan, 1961, 1981), especially chapter 14.

6. See Rowland Smith, "Allan Quatermain to Rosa Burger: Violence in South African Fiction," *World Literature Written in English* 22, no. 2 (1983): 171–182, for a discussion of the literary style of the imperial hero and how Schreiner produced a "model for white liberal scorn of the imperial mode at the same time that Haggard was celebrating it" (172).

7. Stephen Gray, "The Trooper at the Hanging Tree," *English in Africa* 2, no. 2 (September 1975); reprinted in *Olive Schreiner,* ed. Cherry Clayton.

8. Peter Wilhelm discusses J. M. Coetzee's *Dusklands* as a further exploration of the colonizing mission and its relationship with sexual excess in "*Peter Halket*, Rhodes and Colonialism," collected in *Olive Schreiner*, ed. Cherry Clayton (*CB*: 208–211).

9. See Angus Fletcher, *Allegory: The Theory of a Symbolic Mode* (Ithaca: Cornell University Press, 1964), 23, 120.

10. See Elizabeth A. Eldredge and Fred Morton, eds., *Slavery in South Africa: Captive Labour on the Dutch Frontier* (Pietermaritzburg: University of Natal Press, 1995).

11. Alex la Guma, *Apartheid: A Collection of Writings on South African Racism by South Africans* (New York: International Publishers, 1978), 13.

12. See Anthony Appiah's discussion of the relationship between social structure and agency in "Agency and the Interests of Theory" in *Consequences of Theory*, eds. Jonathan Arac and Barbara Johnson (Baltimore: Johns Hopkins Press, 1991), 63–90.

13. Olive Schreiner, *Closer Union* (Cape Town, Constitutional Reform Association: Rustica Press, 1960).

14. See O. Mannoni, *Prospero and Caliban: The Psychology of Colonization*, 1950 (New York: Praeger, 1964) and A. Memmi, *The Colonizer and the Colonized* (New York: Orion Press, 1965).

Chapter Seven

1. I have discussed some of the aspects of the Cronwright-Schreiner marriage in "Olive Schreiner in Johannesburg," *The English Academy Review* 1 (1983): 65–82.

2. Carol Gilligan, *In a Different Voice: Psychological Theory and Women's Development* (Cambridge, Mass.: Harvard University Press, 1982).

3. The story of the impact of the Land Act is told by Sol Plaatje in *Native Life in South Africa Before and Since the European War and the Boer Rebellion* (London: P. S. King and Son, 1916; Braamfontein: Ravan Press, 1982).

4. Vera Brittain, "The Influence of Olive Schreiner," in *Until the Heart Changes: A Garland for Olive Schreiner,* ed. Zelda Friedlander (Cape Town: Tafelberg, 1967), 125–27, 126.

Selected Bibliography

This bibliography is by no means comprehensive and is intended as a list of recommended readings.

PRIMARY SOURCES

A Letter on the Jew. Cape Town: H. Liberman, 1906.

An English South African's View of the Situation: Words in Season. London: Hodder and Stoughton, 1899.

Closer Union. London: Fifield, 1909. Republished with a foreword by Donald Molteno. Cape Town: Constitutional Reform Association, 1960.

Diamond Fields: Only a Story of Course. Fragment of a manuscript introduced by Richard Rive, *English in Africa* 1, no. 1 (March 1974): 3–29.

Dreams. London: Unwin, 1890.

Dream Life and Real Life. By "Ralph Iron." London: Unwin, 1893.

From Man to Man (or *Perhaps Only....*). Introduced by S. C. Cronwright-Schreiner. London: Unwin, 1926. Republished with an introduction by Paul Foot. London: Virago, 1985.

My Other Self: The Letters of Olive Schreiner and Havelock Ellis: 1884–1920. Edited by Yaffa Claire Draznin. New York: Peter Lang, 1992.

Olive Schreiner: Letters 1871–99. Edited by Richard Rive with historical research by Russell Martin. Cape Town: David Philip, 1987.

Stories, Dreams and Allegories. Introduced S. C. Cronwright-Schreiner. London: Unwin, 1923.

The Political Situation. Copublished with S. C. Cronwright-Schreiner. London: Unwin, 1896.

The Story of an African Farm, A Novel. 2 vols. by "Ralph Iron." London: Chapman and Hall, 1883. References are to the Ad Donker edition, introduced by Cherry Clayton, Johannesburg: Ad Donker, 1986.

The Letters of Olive Schreiner. Ed. S. C. Cronwright-Schreiner. London: Unwin, 1924.

Thoughts on South Africa. London: Unwin, 1923. Republished with a foreword by Richard Rive, Johannesburg: Africana Book Society, 1976. References are to the new edition introduced and annotated by Margaret Lenta. Johannesburg: Ad Donker, 1992.

Trooper Peter Halket of Mashonaland. London: Unwin, 1897. Republished with an introduction by Marion Friedmann and the original frontispiece. Johannesburg: Ad Donker, 1974. References are to the recent edition introduced by Sally-Ann Murray. Johannesburg: Ad Donker, 1992.

Undine. Introduced by S. C. Cronwright-Schreiner. London: Benn, 1929.

Woman and Labour. London: Unwin, 1911. References are to the Virago edition with a preface by Jane Graves. London: Virago: 1978.

Manuscript Collections

More detailed information about manuscript collections is to be found in Karel Schoeman's *Olive Schreiner: A Woman in South Africa: 1855–1881*, in Rive and Martin's *Olive Schreiner: Letters 1871–99*, and in Joyce Avrech Berkman's *The Healing Imagination of Olive Schreiner*.

Albany Library, 1820 Settlers Memorial division, Grahamstown, South Africa.
Cory Library, Rhodes University, Grahamstown, South Africa.
Cullen Library, University of the Witwatersrand, Johannesburg.
Edward Carpenter Collection, City Library, Sheffield.
Harry Ransom Humanities Research Center, University of Texas at Austin.
Karl Pearson Papers, University College Library, London, UK.
National English Literary Museum, Grahamstown, South Africa.
Olive Schreiner Collection, J. W. Jagger Library, University of Cape Town.
Olive Schreiner Papers, South African Library, Cape Town.
Strange Collection, Public Library, Johannesburg.

SECONDARY SOURCES

Books and Parts of Books

Albinski, Nan Bowman. " 'The Law of Justice, of Nature, and of Right': Victorian Feminist Utopias." In *Feminism, Utopia, and Narrative*, ed. Libby Falk Jones and Sarah Webster Goodwin, 50–68. Knoxville: University of Tennessee Press, 1990.
Barash, Carol. *An Olive Schreiner Reader.* London: Pandora, 1987.
Barash, Carol L. "Virile Womanhood: Olive Schreiner's Narratives of a Master Race." In *Speaking of Gender*, ed. Elaine Showalter, 269–281. New York: Routledge, 1989.
Beeton, D. R. *Olive Schreiner: A Short Guide to her Writings.* Cape Town: Timmins, 1974.
————. *Portraits of Olive Schreiner: A Manuscript Sourcebook.* Johannesburg: Ad. Donker, 1983.
Beeton, Ridley. *Facets of Olive Schreiner: A Manuscript Source Book.* Johannesburg: Ad Donker, 1987.
Berkman, Joyce Avrech. *Olive Schreiner: Feminism on the Frontier.* St. Albans: Eden, 1979.
————. *The Healing Imagination of Olive Schreiner: Beyond South African Colonialism.* Amherst: University of Massachusetts Press, 1989.
Bjorhovde, Gerd. *Rebellious Structures: Women Writers and the Crisis of the Novel: 1880–1900.* Oslo: Norwegian University Press, 1987.

Blake, Kathleen. *"Olive Schreiner: Art and the Artist Self-Postponed."* In *Love and the Woman Question in Victorian Literature: The Art of Self-Postponement*, 202–27. Sussex: The Harvester Press, 1983.

Clayton, Cherry, ed. *Olive Schreiner.* Johannesburg: Ad Donker, 1983.

———. "Olive Schreiner: Approaches to Her Writing through Biography and Autobiography." In *Autobiographical and Biographical Writing in the Commonwealth*, ed. D. MacDermott, 49–56. Barcelona: Sabadell, 1985.

———. "Olive Schreiner and Katherine Mansfield: Artistic Transformations of the Outcast Figure by Two Colonial Women Writers." In *Short Fiction in the New Literatures in English*, ed. J. Bardolph, 31–39. Nice: Faculté des Lettres et Sciences Humaines, 1989.

———. "Olive Schreiner: Paradoxical Pioneer." In *Women and Writing in South Africa: A Critical Anthology*, ed. Cherry Clayton, 41–59. Marshalltown: Heinemann, 1989.

Cronwright-Schreiner, S. C. *The Life of Olive Schreiner.* London: Fisher-Unwin, 1924.

Donaldson, Laura E. *Decolonizing Feminisms: Race, Gender & Empire-Building.* Chapel Hill: University of North Carolina Press, 1992.

Driver, Dorothy. "Women and Nature, Women as Objects of Exchange: Towards a Feminist Analysis of South African Literature." In *Perspectives on South African English Literature*, ed. Michael Chapman, Colin Gardner, and Es'kia Mphahlele, 454–74. Johannesburg: Ad Donker, 1992.

Du Plessis, Rachel Blau. *Writing Beyond the Ending: Narrative Strategies of Twentieth Century Women Writers.* Bloomington: Indiana University Press, 1985.

First, Ruth, and Ann Scott. *Olive Schreiner.* London: Deutsch, 1980.

Friedlander, Zelda, ed. *Until the Heart Changes: A Garland for Olive Schreiner.* Cape Town: Tafelberg, 1967.

Gray, Stephen. "Schreiner and the Novel Tradition." In *Southern African Literature: An Introduction*, 133–59. Cape Town: David Philip, 1979.

Heywood, Christopher. "Olive Schreiner's Influence on George Moore and D. H. Lawrence." In *Aspects of South African Literature*, ed. Christopher Heywood, 42–53. London: Heinemann, 1976.

Horton, Susan. *Difficult Women, Artful Lives: Olive Schreiner and Isak Dinesen in and out of Africa.* Baltimore: Johns Hopkins Press, 1995.

Kaarsholm, Preben. "The Significance of Evolutionism in Olive Schreiner's *African Farm.*" In *A Sense of Place: Essays in Post-Colonial Literatures*, ed. Britta Olinder, 204–9. Gothenburg: Gothenburg University Press, 1984.

McClintock, Anne. "Olive Schreiner: The Limits of Colonial Feminism." In her *Imperial Leather: Race, Gender and Sexuality in the Colonial Context*, 258–95. London: Routledge, 1995.

Middleton, Victoria. "Doris Lessing's Debt to Olive Schreiner." In *Doris Lessing: The Alchemy of Survival*, ed. Carey Kaplan and Ellen Cronan Rose, 135–47. Athens: Ohio University Press, 1988.

Monsman, Gerald. "A Child on the Farm." In *International Literature in English: Essays on the Major Writers*, ed. Robert L. Ross, 5–19. New York: Garland, 1991.

———. *Olive Schreiner's Fiction: Landscape and Power*. New Brunswick: Rutgers University Press, 1991.

Schoeman, Karel. *Olive Schreiner: A Woman in South Africa 1855–1881*. Johannesburg: Jonathan Ball, 1991.

———. *Only an Anguish to Live Here: Olive Schreiner and the Anglo-Boer War 1899–1902*. Cape Town: Human & Rousseau, 1992.

Showalter, Elaine. *Gender and Culture at the Fin de Siècle*. London: Bloomsbury: 1991.

Smith, Malvern van Wyk, and Don Maclennan, eds. *Olive Schreiner and After: Essays on Southern African Literature in Honour of Guy Butler*. Cape Town: David Philip, 1983.

Spender, Dale. "Interdependence: Olive Schreiner." In her *Women of Ideas*, 646–656. London: Routledge, 1983.

Stanley, Liz. "Olive Schreiner: New Women, Free Women, All Women." In *Feminist Theorists: Three Centuries of Women's Intellectual Traditions*, ed. Dale Spender, 229–243. London: The Women's Press, 1983.

Stubbs, Patricia. *Women and Fiction: Feminism and the Novel, 1880–1920*. London: The Harvester Press, 1979.

Vivan, Itala, ed. *The Flawed Diamond: Essays on Olive Schreiner*. Sydney: Dangaroo Press, 1989.

Wade, Michael. *White on Black in South Africa: A Study of English-Language Inscriptions of Skin Colour*. London: Macmillan, 1993.

Winkler, Barbara Scott, "Victorian Daughters: The Lives and Feminism of Charlotte Perkins Gilman and Olive Schreiner." In *Critical Essays on Charlotte Perkins Gilman*, ed. Joanne B. Karpinski, 173–83. New York: G. K. Hall, 1992.

Journal Articles

Ayling, Ronald. "Literature of the Eastern Cape from Schreiner to Fugard." *Ariel* 16, no. 2 (April 1985): 77–98.

Barsby, Christine. "Olive Schreiner: Towards a Redefinition of Culture." *Pretexts* 1, no. 1 (Winter 1989): 18–39.

Bolin, Bill. "Olive Schreiner and the Status Quo." *UNISA English Studies* 31, no. 1 (April 1993): 4–8.

Bradford, Helen. "Introducing Palinsky Smith." *English in Africa* 21, nos. 1 and 2 (July 1994): 1–32. (Contains previously unavailable early sketches by Olive Schreiner, published when she first arrived in England.)

Casey, Janet Galligani. "Power, Agency, Desire: Olive Schreiner and the Pre-Modern Narrative Moment." *Narrative* 4, no. 2 (May 1996): 124–141.

Clayton, Cherry. "Women Writers and the Law of the Father: Race and Gender in the Fiction of Olive Schreiner, Pauline Smith and Sarah Gertrude Millin." *English Academy Review* 7 (1990): 99–117.

Coetzee, J. M. "Farm Novel and Plaasroman in South Africa." *English in Africa* 13, no. 2 (October 1986): 1–19. Reprinted in his *White Writing: On the Culture of Letters in South Africa*, 63–81. New Haven: Yale University Press, 1988.

Donaldson, Laura. "(Ex)Changing (Wo)Man: Towards a Materialist-Feminist Semiotics." *Cultural Critique* 11 (Winter 1988–1989): 5–23.

Fradkin, Betty McGinnis. "Olive Schreiner and Karl Pearson." *Quarterly Bulletin of the South African Library* 31, no. 4 (1977): 83–93.

———. "Havelock Ellis and Olive Schreiner's 'Gregory Rose.' " *Texas Quarterly* 21, no. 3 (1978): 145–53.

Friedmann, Marion V. *Olive Schreiner: A Study in Latent Meanings.* Johannesburg: University of Witwatersrand Press, 1955.

Gorak, Irene E. "Olive Schreiner's Colonial Allegory: 'The Story of an African Farm.' " *Ariel* 23, no. 4 (October 1992): 53–72.

Green, G. V. "Overturning the Doll's House: A Feminist Comparison between Olive Schreiner's *The Story of an African Farm* and Miles Franklin's *My Brilliant Career*." *Crux* 17, no. 2 (May 1983): 47–59.

Haynes, R. D. "Elements of Romanticism in *The Story of an African Farm*." *English Literature in Transition* 24, no. 2 (1981): 59–79.

Jacob, Susan. "Sharers in a Common Hell: The Colonial Text in Schreiner, Conrad and Lessing." *The Literary Criterion* 23, no. 4 (1988): 84–92.

Lenta, Margaret. "Independence as the Creative Choice in Two South African Fictions." *Ariel* 17, no. 1 (January 1986): 35–52.

———. "Racism, Sexism, and Olive Schreiner's Fiction." *Theoria* 70 (October 1987): 15–30.

Lewis, Simon. "Atavism and the European History of Africa." *Ariel* 27, no. 1 (January 1996): 41–60.

Marcus, Jane. "Olive Schreiner: Cartographer of the Spirit." *The Minnesota Review* 12 (1979): 58–66.

Marquard, Jean. "Hagar's Child: A Reading of *The Story of an African Farm*." *Standpunte* 29, no.1 (1976): 35–47.

———. "Olive Schreiner's 'Prelude': The Child as Artist." *English Studies in Africa* 22, no. 1 (March 1979): 1–11.

Monsman, Gerald. "Patterns of Narration and Characterization in Schreiner's *The Story of an African Farm*." *English Literature in Transition* 28, no. 3 (1985): 253–70.

———. "The Idea of 'Story' In Olive Schreiner's *Story of an African Farm*." *Texas Studies in Literature and Language* 27, no. 3 (Fall 1985): 249–69.

———. "Olive Schreiner: Literature and the Politics of Power." *Texas Studies in Literature and Language* 30, no. 4 (Winter 1988): 583–610.

————. "Olive Schreiner's Allegorical Vision." *Victorian Review* 18, no. 2 (Winter 1992): 49–62.

————. "Writing the Self on the Imperial Frontier: Olive Schreiner and the Stories of Africa." *Bucknell Review* 37, no. 1 (1993): 134–55.

Ogede, Ode. "The Tragic Vision in Olive Schreiner's *The Story of an African Farm*." *Kuka* (1980–1981): 26–33.

Paxton, Nancy L. "*The Story of an African Farm* and the Dynamics of Woman-to-Woman Influence." *Texas Studies in Literature and Language* 30, no. 4 (1988): 562–82.

Pechey, Graham. "*The Story of an African Farm*: Colonial History and the Discontinuous Text." *Critical Arts* 3, no. 1 (1983): 65–78.

Ross, Robert. "A New Time for the Fiction of Sarah Gertrude Millin and Olive Schreiner." *World Literature Written in English* 24, no. 2 (1984): 239–43.

Sarvan, C. P. "Olive Schreiner's *Trooper Peter Halket*: An Altered Awareness." *International Fiction Review* 11, no. 1 (Winter 1984): 45–46.

Style, Colin. "Olive Schreiner Today." *Contemporary Review* 244, no. 1419 (April 1984): 204–9.

Scherzinger, Karen. "The Problem of the Pure Woman: South African Pastoralism and Female Rites of Passage." *UNISA English Studies* 29, no. 2 (September 1991): 29–35.

Visel, Robin. " 'We Bear the World and We Make It': Bessie Head and Olive Schreiner." *Research in African Literatures* 21, no. 3 (Fall 1990): 115–24.

Voss, A. E. "A Generic Approach to the South African Novel in English." *UCT Studies in English* 7 (September 1977): 110–11.

Voss, Tony. "Avatars of Waldo." *Alternation* 1, no. 2 (1994): 15–25.

Walkowitz, Judith R. "Science, Feminism and Romance: The Men and Women's Club." *History Workshop Journal* 21 (Spring 1986): 37–59.

Wilkinson, Jane. "Dust and Dew. Moonlight and Utopia. Natural Imagery in the First South African Novel." *Commonwealth Essays and Studies* 14, no. 2 (Spring 1992): 34–43.

Index

The Author

Cherry Clayton was born and educated in South Africa and completed her Ph.D. on Olive Schreiner at the University of Natal in 1985. She taught at the University of the Witwatersrand and was Associate Professor of English at Rand Afrikaans University in Johannesburg before moving to Canada in 1990. She currently teaches English and women's studies at the University of Guelph, Ontario. She has published a critical anthology of feminist essays, *Women and Writing in South Africa: A Critical Anthology* (Johannesburg: Heinemann, 1989), and a collection of interviews with South African women writers, *Between the Lines: Interviews with Bessie Head, Sheila Roberts, Ellen Kuzwayo, Miriam Tlali* (Grahamstown: NELM, 1989). She has edited *Olive Schreiner's "Thoughts about Woman"* (Pretoria: State Library, 1985) and *The Woman's Rose* (Johannesburg: Ad. Donker, 1986), a selection of Schreiner's stories and allegories. She has also written a new introduction to *The Story of an African Farm* (Johannesburg: Ad. Donker, 1986) and edited a casebook of primary and secondary materials about Schreiner, *Olive Schreiner* (Johannesburg: McGraw-Hill, 1983). In addition, she has published poetry and short stories in journals and South African anthologies. Her first collection of poetry, *Leaving Home*, appeared in 1994. Current research involves a project on gender and culture in relation to the political transformation of South Africa.